The Power of Agreement

The Power of Agreement

© Copyright 2009, Daryl C.J. Allen

ISBN 978-0-578-01369-5

All rights reserved

Lulu Enterprises, Inc.
860 Aviation Parkway, Suite 300
Morrisville, NC 27560
www.lulu.com

All scriptures are quoted from various versions of the Holy Bible. I intentionally put satan's name in small letters because I chose not to exalt him in any way even to the extent of being grammatically incorrect.

Prepare The Way Ministries
revdcja@yahoo.com

The Table of Contents

Chapter 1
The Power in Agreement

Can two walk together, except they be agreed?
Amos 3:3

Years ago, the Lord began dealing with me about being a man of integrity. He told me there were some things He wanted me to resolve in my life that spoke of my level of integrity as a man of God. In short, God wanted me to be a man of my word. I have this saying, *"a man is no greater than his word."* And based upon that slogan I wasn't much of a man at that time when it came to certain unresolved matters in my personal life.

One of those unresolved matters in my life was my student loan. At a certain point in my life prior to my living wholly for God, I went to school through a student loan. After I graduated, I neglected to maintain my payments on the loan and eventually stopped altogether. Years later as I grew in the Lord, God said to me, *you need to resume your payments on your student loan.*

Needless to say, I repented to God for my negligence. I called the loan center and apologize to them for my negligence as well and asked if I could set up a payment plan to get this loan paid off. They agreed to get everything reestablished and set me up on a payment plan. Payments were difficult to maintain because I was on disability at the time. But I knew I had to obey God and allow Him to develop godly character, faith, and integrity within me in this and other areas of my life.

Well, after a few years of being faithful in my payments, God's favor kicked in. My credit was restored and not long after, because of my disability, the loan center forgave me of the loan and informed me I no longer needed to make payments. Hallelujah.

The Power of Agreement

In this simple process God began to really give me revelation on the importance of agreement. It wasn't about my loan. It wasn't about my challenges in making the payments. And it wasn't about my credit. It was about agreement.

You and I enter into agreements every day. Some knowingly and some unknowingly. Some spiritual and some natural. Some on paper and some with a handshake. Some with words and some with a nod of the head or with the wink of an eye.

Right, wrong, good, bad, or indifferent, we come into agreement with something or someone every single day of our lives.

The word agreement is defined as, *the willingness to walk in a set of plans & standards.*

Can two walk together, except they be agreed?
Amos 3:3

So with this definition, we can see that walking together isn't just a matter of physically walking together in a park or to the store. It is a decision that causes the parties involved to make the plans and set the standards that becomes a part of their lives. And in agreeing with these plans and standards, they dictate the course of their lives and the perception of those who are associated with us.

Agreement is powerful. It is a characteristic we seldom think about but is a major aspect of life and our spiritual walk. Agreement is not just a one-time experience, but a consistent unconscious mindset we walk in at all times and encounter on countless occasions.

Agreement is unbiased. What ever we agree with becomes a part of us either temporal or for a lifetime.

And the more we come into agreement, the more we become what we agree with until we are what we agree with.

Looking at the above scripture, we need to examine carefully two words of this passage. The two are, *"walk together."* Walking together shows a willingness to be with and/or involved. Thus we see the passage in full view, walking in agreement. Walking in agreement shows a willingness to exert physical, emotional, and mental strength to go in a direction both parties are comfortable with or willing to go. Therefore the question that arises is who decides the direction the two parties involved are going. The answer is usually the one which has the most power and influence is the one who decides and directs the other on the course to be traveled.

Whoever is more power or influential controls the destiny of the other. Whether good or evil, if the influence and power of the one leading is effective enough, they can turn an entire nation or world in the direction they desire. Adolf Hitler, Jim Jones, Martin Luther King Jr., Mahatma Ghandi, and last but certainly not least, the Lord Jesus Christ. All these men had (in Christ's case, have) the power and the influence to turn the hearts of people to agree with their convictions, and even die for them. And even to this day many people are still living in agreement with those who have long since died. This is the power in agreement.

Agreement is a process. The process of agreement depends upon our level of willingness and yieldedness to either the spirit or the flesh or with God or satan.

Now as a believer, you might say, I don't agree with satan. But I say as long as we have flesh operating in our lives, we have a doorway for the enemy. The fear in this is we're not always in control of our flesh and thus not always aware when the enemy is operating through us.

5

The Power of Agreement

This is why God puts emphasis on killing the flesh. When the flesh is completely crucified, the enemy's access in our lives and ministries will be completely shut down. And if our flesh is crucified, we cease to commit sin and God has free course in our lives and can use us more effectively for His glory. Thus, we are no longer in agreement with the influence and trappings of satan, sin, and death, but in agreement with God, holiness, and eternal life.

Knowing this, that our old man is crucified with him, that the body of sin might be destroyed, that henceforth we should not serve sin. For he that is dead is freed from sin
Romans 6:6,7

The key to agreement is the power to choose. We chose to accept Jesus Christ as our personal Lord and Savior. We choose to live in accordance with His will and His word on a daily basis. We chose to renounce the sin life and live a life of holiness and righteousness in the sight of God. We chose to walk away from a life that was leading us to hell. And we choose to suffer for the cause of Christ. The more we choose to walk with Lord Jesus, the more we choose to live and move and have our being in His Spirit, the more we become like Lord Jesus.

Choose you this day whom ye will serve; whether the gods which your fathers served that were on the other side of the flood, or the gods of the Amorites, in whose land ye dwell: but as for me and my house, we will serve the Lord
Joshua 24:15

6

As I mentioned earlier, agreement is a process. But the foundation of the process in serving God is making the right choices according to God's word and the leading of the Holy Spirit on a daily basis that we might be conformed to the image of Jesus Christ. It is God's greatest desire we become like Lord Jesus and the season is coming that those who've made the right choices will see the fullness of God in their lifetime.

> *For whom He did foreknow, He also did*
> *predestinate to be conformed to the image of*
> *His Son, that He might be the firstborn among*
> *many brethren*
> *Romans 8:28*

God has predestinated us to be conformed to the image of Lord Jesus. But just because we are predestinated doesn't mean it will come to pass. We must come into agreement with the process that comes with being conformed.

Many people feel that just because we are called to do things for God and God has promised to bless us it is just going to happen without any involvement from us. This is not accurate teaching. Remember the scripture mentioned earlier?

> *How can two walk together, except they be agreed?*
> *Amos 3:3*

There are many things God wants to do in our lives, but if we don't come into agreement with the will of God for those things to manifest in our lives then we are in danger of forfeiting the promises of God.

7

The Power of Agreement

We hear people say things like, *"well, if it's the Lord's will, it will happen."* It's the will of God that all be saved but we don't see this happening. It's the will of God that we all be healed and delivered but we don't see this happening either. It all comes down to making the choice to **agree and to do** the will of God so we can see the will and glory of God come forth in our lives (James 1:22-24).

Agreement can be temporal or last a lifetime. Salvation doesn't just save us from going to hell. It reveals to us that we've been living a lie.

> *But if our gospel be hid, it is hid to them that are lost: In whom the god of this world hath blinded the minds of them which believe not, lest the light of the glorious gospel of Christ, who is the image of God, should shine unto them*
> *II Corinthians 4:3,4*

Many things we've become comfortable with before salvation, when we encounter the cross through the preaching of the true, full gospel, we've come to suddenly realize that this life we've been living was not the way it was supposed to be. We realize the life we've lived was a ploy by the devil to keep us blind to the truth that there is more to this life than what we've been living and the only way to realize this is through Jesus Christ (John 14:6).

Once we have accepted Christ, we are faced with the challenge of letting go of the life we have been in agreement with for many years. Some things we are able to let go immediately. Others may take months or even years. Not that we refuse to let go, but that they have become so much a part of us, we just don't know how, or want to.

8

Agreement can be a taskmaster. It can be tormenting and condemning but it can also be wonderful, powerful, and life changing. Concerning the negative aspect of agreement, we want to let go of it. But to get free will take renouncing the negative agreement, and agreeing with the power and the word of God to get free, and a daily resolve to forsake this bondage in order to fully embrace that which is lovely, true, pure, honest, and of a good report (Philippians 4:8).

> *And it shall come to pass in that day, that his burden shall be taken away from off thy shoulder, and his yoke from off thy neck, and the yoke shall be destroyed because of the anointing...For with God nothing shall be impossible*
> *Isaiah 10:27; Luke 1:37*

What ever we do, we should never give up seeking God to release us from that which is designed to destroy our lives and relationship with Lord Jesus. Don't give up no matter what because your life depends on it.

Agreement in prayer is powerful. Prayer is, next to the power to choose, the Holy Spirit and the word of God, the most powerful instrument we have to fulfilling the will of God on earth. But it is the most abused instrument in the kingdom of God. Someone once said, *"When you don't understand the purpose of a thing, you will abuse it."* This is so true for some of us concerning prayer.

There are 2 important aspects of agreement when it comes to prayer we must understand for it to be affective in our lives and ministries. The first is we must *come into agreement with the Holy Spirit.* Prayer cannot be conducted effectively and fulfilled apart from the Spirit of God.

9

The Power of Agreement

 It is so important that we as believers understand that prayer is powerful only when the Holy Spirit is leading and conducting the praying through us.

Likewise the Spirit also helpeth our infirmities: for we know not what we should pray for as we ought: but the Spirit itself maketh intercession for us with groanings which cannot be uttered. And he that searcheth the hearts knoweth what is the mind of the Spirit, because he maketh intercession for the saints according to the will of God
Romans 8:26,27

Submitting (agreeing) to the leading of God-the Holy Spirit in prayer is vital if the will of God is going to be done in the earth (John 15:1-5). If God-the Holy Spirit is not orchestrating our prayer time, we are like Nadab and Abihu offering up strange fire through our fleshly petitions to God (Leviticus 10:1). And we know there is no good thing, which can come from this (Romans 7:18; 8:8).

Before we pray, we can request for God to reveal his will He wishes for us to lift up to Him (whether it be personal or for someone else). Once we know God is using us in Spirit-led prayer we can expect our faith to be built up and our prayers to be answered in the time God has ordained (Matthew 10:19,20).

The second aspect of agreement in prayer is *the response to our prayers from those who are the subject of our prayers*. I pray what I am about to share sets many of you free concerning prayer. Many times we've become discouraged and have even given up in our prayers for loved ones and those issues that are heavy on our hearts.

The reason behind these feelings of futility is because there are no visible changes one way or another to that or to whom our prayers are directed. Let me say to you, this does not mean you were not praying the will of God nor is it implying that God wasn't hearing your prayers. God will give those we're praying for thoughts, emotional unction in their hearts, speak to them in their dreams, send someone to speak with them, or even set up natural circumstances to lead them in the direction God, through our prayers, would have them to go. But if that person or people who are the object of our prayers refuse to respond to the leading of the Holy Spirit, then God will not violate their will. We must be sensitive enough to the Lord to hear Him say, "I release you. Don't pray anymore for them." Because at some point God will no longer attempt to influence a heart that is hard towards Him (Hebrews 3:12).

We must have constant communication with God-the Holy Spirit to know that we are doing the Lord's will. This will release us from questions concerning the validity of our prayer-life and relationship with God or the accuracy of our prayers. It takes the people we're praying for to come into agreement with the answer God sends to them through our prayer.

But we must also know the timing of God concerning prayer. Don't put an expiration date on your prayers. God will answer them according to His plan and in His time. Our responsibility is to only pray according to the will of God. It's God's responsibility to answer our prayers and it's the people's responsibility to respond to the answer from God. God will only judge us whether we have prayed His will. He will judge the people based upon their response to the prayer. This should bring peace to those of us who have been crying out to God for years. I pray that it does.

The Power of Agreement

Agreement releases the power of God-the Holy Spirit in our lives. It is the divine power of God-the Holy Spirit that has given us everything we need to fulfill our destiny. The key to fulfilling our destiny and walking in the full character of Lord Jesus is agreeing with the power of the Holy Spirit that dwells and works within each believer.

> *Now unto him that is able to do exceeding*
> *abundantly above all that we ask or think,*
> *according to* **the power that worketh in us**
> *Ephesians 3:20*

The power of God has the ability to provide us with anything we need at any given time. It all depends upon how much of the power we are allowing to work in and through us. Remember the earth belongs to God and everyone and everything is at His disposal. But if we limit God by not yielding to Him then we cannot receive the blessings of God.

> *Nevertheless they did flatter him with their*
> *mouth, and they lied unto him with their*
> *tongues. For their heart was not right with him,*
> *neither were they stedfast in his covenant.*
> *...How oft did they provoke him in the*
> *wilderness, and grieve him in the desert! Yea,*
> *they turned back and tempted God, and limited*
> *the Holy One of Israel. They remembered not*
> *his hand, nor the day when he delivered them*
> *from the enemy.*
> *Psalm 78:36,37, 40-42*

I encourage you to read this psalm. I believe it will be an eye-opener as it relates to how we may be limiting God.

The two words that make the journey of Israel so tragic is *"they forgot."* They forgot all of the wonderful things God did for them in Egypt. They forgot the signs and wonders He performed in bringing them out of bondage. They forgot how He provided for them and kept them healthy, warm, and safe from the inhabitants of the land while wondering in the wilderness. And because they forgot what God did for them to build their faith, they limited God.

The word limit in Hebrew means, *to vex, grieve, and irritate.* Hopefully this will put what Israel did and possibly what you and I may be doing to God in a more sobering perspective. Because when we equate this to what we're doing in not obeying God, we vex, grieve, and irritate to Lord our God.

The history of Israel is supposed to be our teacher. Not for us to repeat it. We must shake off the spirits of our spiritual and natural ancestors and begin a new trend of faith, obedience, and commitment to our God.

> *Moreover, brethren, I would not that ye should*
> *be ignorant, how that all our fathers were under*
> *the cloud, and all passed through the sea; And*
> *were all baptized unto Moses in the cloud and*
> *in the sea; And did all eat the same spiritual*
> *meat; And did all drink the same spiritual drink:*
> *for they drank of that spiritual Rock that*
> *followed them: and that Rock was Christ. But*
> *with many of them God was not well pleased:*
> *for they were overthrown in the wilderness.*
> *Now these things were our examples, to the*
> *intent we should not lust after evil things, as*
> *they also lusted*
> *I Corinthians 10:1-6*

The Power of Agreement

All we need can only be obtained when we come into agreement with God and walk the narrow path He has chosen for us. When we consistently agree with the will of God concerning us the greater our opportunity to experience the fullness of God and fulfill our destiny for the good of the kingdom and for the glory of our God.

If ye be willing and obedient, ye shall eat the
good of the land
Isaiah 1:19

Chapter 2
The importance of identification

One of the most important and probably one of the most frightening and challenging questions a father hears from their child is, *"who am I."* A child at some point in their development instinctively looks for identification. We fathers are given a great responsibility of imparting identity to our children. In receiving identity from the father, a sense of authority is imparted to the child. This is evident when we hear our children say, *"my daddy told me that I was going to be a..."*

Now to the ladies whom have been so courageous and successful in raising children on their own, I mean no disrespect or to demean your efforts. I merely speak from a biblical perspective that we fathers are given responsibility by God to give identity to our offspring. It is unfortunate in the day that we live in it is unfortunate that fatherless children must turn to their mothers to receive identity. In today's belief systems, this may sound offensive, but it is true. But God has caused it to work for our good.

Identity produces a sense of belonging. It creates structure and establishes principles in the lives of our children. It gives them a sense of adventure to fulfill what the father has spoken over them. When the hands of fatherly authority is laid upon the child, that identity spoken is released into their hearts and a resolve to see these words fulfilled overtakes the mind and heart of the child.

A psychological definition for identification is, *a largely unconscious process whereby an individual models thoughts, feelings, and actions after those attributed to an object that has been incorporated as a mental image.*

Where there is no vision, the people perish...
Proverbs 29:18a
15

The Power of Agreement

When you impart identity your are releasing a mental image into the mind of the person to whom it is directed. It is a psychological blueprint planted in the mind of individuals to give direction and purpose. The more this identification is practiced the more the person assumes this identity as a lifestyle rather than an idea.

Give instruction to a youth about his way, Even
when he is old he turneth not from it
Proverbs 22:6
1898 Young's Literal Translation

The Greek meanings for agreement are *Resemblance or Possession.* I stated earlier, the more we come into agreement, the more we become what we agree with or the more we resemble what we've come into agreement with.

This is simply because what we have agreed with has possessed us so much so that our thinking and behavior are completely transformed by the image imparted to us.

Know ye not, that to whom ye yield yourselves
servants to obey, his servants ye are to whom
ye obey; whether of sin unto death, or of
obedience unto righteousness?
Romans 6:16

This is why it is so vitally important that we impart identity into the heart of a child at the earliest age possible because at that age the child is completely open to instruction and direction. The older they get and the more they experience, the more difficult it is to set their feet on the path they're created to walk. This is why God says we must become as little children. We must unlearn in order to learn.

The importance of identification

There are 2 entities we come into agreement with and they are God and satan. There are 2 ways by which we come into agreement with God or satan. They are, if we come into agreement with God, it is by of our spirit-man through the influence of God-the Holy Spirit and the studying of and living according to the word of truth. And if we come into agreement with satan, it is by way of our flesh as he influences us through the pleasures of sin and the things of the world.

There is no gray area in this principle. Either God influences us as we walk in the spirit or satan influences us when we walk in our flesh. And which ever we come into agreement and practice more becomes predominant in our lives and ministries.

*Know ye not, that to whom ye yield yourselves
servants to obey, his servants ye are to whom
ye obey; whether of sin unto death, or of
obedience unto righteousness...For they that
are after the flesh do mind the things of the
flesh; but they that are after the Spirit the
things of the Spirit.
Romans 6:16; Romans 8:5*

One of the keys of agreement is allowing that which you're agreeing with to possess you. This level of possession becomes so great, we resemble the very one we've come into agreement with. With that being said, I want to share with you some real life accounts of men and women who came into agreement with the identity of Christ and walked in the power and demonstration of the Spirit. They yielded to will of the Father and submitted to the presence of the Holy Spirit and allowed Him to use them as He saw fit.

17

The Power of Agreement

These men and women of God received their identity as the hand of Almighty God was laid upon them and He told them who they were. The words of God spoken into their hearts so consumed them they gave up all to assume the very identity God revealed to them. And just as they gave up all to receive their Godly identity, so should we that we may receive our identity in Christ. The only way you and I can demonstrate what you're about to read can only be done by a willingness to give up one's own will to take on the identity of Christ to touch millions by and for the glory of God.

John Wesley

As Wesley preached, the power of God often came upon his listeners, and hundreds would fall under the power of the Holy Spirit. Then, in answer, to prayer their souls and bodies were healed. A physician became offended at the cries of many who fell under the power of God. He attended Wesley's meeting and a lady he knew fell under the power. "Great drops of sweat ran down her face, and all her bones shook. But when both her soul and body were healed in a moment he acknowledged the finger of God."

Charles G. Finney

"Finney seemed so anointed with the Holy Spirit that people were often brought under conviction of sin just by looking at him. When holding meetings at Utica, New York, he visited a large factory. At the sight of him one of the workers, and then another, and then another broke down and wept under a sense of their sins, and finally so many were sobbing and weeping that the machinery had to be stopped while Finney pointed them to Christ."

The importance of identification

Smith Wigglesworth

On one occasion, he recalled, "I was traveling to Cardiff in South Wales. I had been much in prayer on the journey. The carriage was full of people whom I knew to be unsaved, but as there was so much talking and joking I could not get in a word for my Master. As the train was nearing the station, I thought I would wash my hands... and as I returned to the carriage, a man jumped up and said, 'Sir, you convince me of sin,' and fell on his knees there and then. Soon the whole carriage of people were crying out the same way. They said, 'Who are you? What are you? You convince us all of sin'..."

John G. Lake

My soul was crying out to God in a yearning too deep for words, when suddenly it seemed to me, that I had passed under a shower of warm tropical rain, which was not falling upon me, but through me. My spirit, and soul and body under this influence soothed into such a deep still calm, as I had never known. My brain, which had always been so active, became perfectly still. An awe of the presence of God settled over me. I knew it was God. "Some moments passed; I do not know how many. The Spirit said, 'I have heard your prayers, I have seen your tears. You are now Baptized in the Holy Spirit.' Then currents of power began to rush through my being from the crown of my head to the soles of my feet. The shocks of power increased in rapidity, and voltage. As these currents of power would pass through me, they seemed to come upon my head, rush through my body, and through my feet into the floor... Even at this late date, the awe of that hour rests upon my soul.

The Power of Agreement

"I found that my life began to manifest in the varied range of the gifts of the Spirit. I spoke in tongues by the power of God, and God flowed through me with a new force. Healings were of a more powerful order. God manifested in me; God spoke through me. My spirit was energized. I had a new comprehension of God's will and a new revelation of God in me. My nature became so sensitized, that I could lay hands on any man, or woman, and tell what organ was diseased, and to what extent, and all about it. I tested it. I went into hospitals where physicians could not diagnose a case, touched a patient, and instantly I knew the organ that was diseased, its extent, condition, and location.

Maria Woodworth-Etter

Reports state that she would come into a town after sleeping in a tent, and within days there would be approximately 20,000 people in her meetings. At times, God would give people working in the fields in a fifty-mile radius around her meetings visions of heaven and hell, and they would fall to the ground under tremendous conviction. It was like a "blanket" anointing that would come down upon the whole area. It has been reported that for blocks around her meetings, people would fall to the ground repenting.

Remember, the definition for identification is, *a largely unconscious process whereby an individual models thoughts, feelings, and actions after those attributed to an object that has been incorporated as a mental image.*

*For whom he did foreknow, he also did predestinate to be conformed to the **image** of his Son...*
Romans 8:29

20

The Importance of Identification

I remember one Sunday in Church, my daughter, Shanah, who is eleven years old, came over and sat on her daddy's lap as the service was coming to a close. As she sat there with me, one of the associate pastors looked at the two of us together and just began to laugh. I noticed his laughter was directed toward us so after the service I asked him, "What we're you laughing about?" He said in a very amusing way, "I looked over at you with your daughter sitting there on your lap and both of you had your heads leaning the same way, you had the same look on your face, and your lips where fixed in the same position." Neither I, nor my daughter, were aware of this posture. Without any effort of any kind, she was acting just like her daddy. "When you agree with the DNA of something or someone you take on their characteristics and become what you've agreed with. My daughter didn't have to think about it, she just did it.

The more you and I come into agreement with Christ, taking on His character and nature, the more we act like Him with literally no effort at all. The more we spend time in His presence, the more we resemble Jesus. The key to this is *the willingness to walk in a set of plans & standards.*

But I say, walk and live [habitually] in the [Holy] Spirit [responsive to and controlled and guided by the Spirit]; then you will certainly not gratify the cravings and desires of the flesh (of human nature without God)...If we live by the [Holy] Spirit, let us also walk by the Spirit, [if by the Holy Spirit we have our life in God, let us go forward walking in line, our conduct controlled by the Spirit.]
Galatians 5:16,25
The Amplified Version

21

The Power of Agreement

The power of agreement is the willingness to identify with an idea or with someone. The reason why we see radical Muslims so willing to strap bombs to themselves and push the button, the reason they're willing to fly airplanes into buildings, is because of their willingness to identify with an ideal called Islam. We know this is a type of anti-christ manifesting in the earth. We know these precious people are severely deceived. But the concept of them identifying so deeply with their belief system that they're willing to die for it is something we as Christians must conduct a personal examination and ask ourselves are we identifying with Christ as deeply as the Muslims are with Islam?

I believe, based upon the word of God, if we were identifying more with Christ, we would see more souls saved, healed, and delivered. We possess the greatest power in the universe-God-the Holy Spirit. If we would only abandon ourselves completely to the will and influence of God-the Holy Spirit, we could completely eradicate every false religious practice, every ungodly belief system, every form of corruption, and all forms of sickness and diseases in the world and then all of mankind would be willing to identify with the Lord our God. But this can only be accomplished by those of us who name the name of Jesus, agreeing with and yielding to, and identifying with the Him.

Chapter 3
Agreement with Reality

The word reality comes from the root word real, which is defined as, *actual rather than imaginary.* In chapter one, I shared with you that the definition of agreement is, *the willingness to walk in a set of plans and standard.* The willingness to walk in a set of plans and standards shape the way we think and function. How I think determines the way I function. In other words, **What we agree with becomes our reality**.

The desktop reference defines reality as *Something that exist or the quality of being factual.* But in many ways, not everything we see, hear, or think is factual or real.

satan is the father of lies. Father, in some translations mean, *source.* He is the source of all forms of deceptions. He creates the lie to appear to be factual or true. Or He adds just enough truth to the lie to make it appear to be true. But it's still a lie. **"No matter how true it sounds or appears, if it's coming from enemy, it's a lie."** The problem is to be able to properly discern that it is a lie because the more we come into agreement and believe the lies of the enemy the more it is entrenched in our hearts. And the more this happens, the more that lie becomes our reality. Once it becomes our reality, we see everything through the eyes of that lie because it has taken control of our perspective and thought life.

The same is true pertaining to God. The more we come into agreement with God-the Holy Spirit and adhere to the word of God, the more God becomes our reality. The more this happens, the more we see and become like Him.

I have heard of thee by the hearing of the ear:
but now mine eye seeth thee
Job 42:5,6

The Power of Agreement

The word that makes this scripture so revelatory is the word *seeth*. This is not just speaking of seeing with the natural eye. It also speaks of properly discerning and perceiving. It speaks of having real life encounters with God through visions, dreams, and His manifested presence.

Now it came to pass in the thirtieth year, in the fourth month, in the fifth day of the month, as I was among the captives by the river of Chebar, that the heavens were opened, and I saw visions of God… Then the spirit took me up, and I heard behind me a voice of a great rushing, saying, Blessed be the glory of the LORD from his place. I heard also the noise of the wings of the living creatures that touched one another, and the noise of the wheels over against them, and a noise of a great rushing. So the spirit lifted me up, and took me away, and I went in bitterness, in the heat of my spirit; but the hand of the LORD was strong upon me. Then I came to them of the captivity at Tel-abib, that dwelt by the river of Chebar, and I sat where they sat, and remained there astonished among them seven days
Ezekiel 1:1; 3:12-15

And Jacob went out from Beer-sheba, and went toward Haran… And he dreamed, and behold a ladder set up on the earth, and the top of it reached to heaven: and behold the angels of God ascending and descending on it. And Jacob awaked out of his sleep, and he said, Surely the LORD is in this place;

and I knew it not. And he was afraid, and said,
How dreadful is this place! this is none other
but the house of God, and this is the gate of
heaven
Genesis 28:10,12,16,17

The more we experience God, the more our reality is transformed to see God in every aspect of life. In short, **"the more I experience God, the more He becomes my reality."** Hearing about God is one thing. Experiencing God is another. **And you can't debate with experience.**

But the question is, **"what is true reality?"** The world is filled with people with varied realities. In every culture we find ourselves in, within that culture there are thousands of men and women living in different realities. And realities are created through various beliefs and experiences.

Even in the family structure, you have a father, a mother, and children. A family united and loving one another still has varied opinions of life. When a person stands before an audience sharing his views, what he's doing is attempting to change people's perspectives whether for good or evil.

So what is true reality? In order to know this we must first come to the conclusion that our reality is not the proper one. When we realize this, we're open to receive what's true. And the only place we can find the right reality is in Christ.

For in him we live, and move, and have our being
Acts 17:28a

Christ is our reality. The more I remain in Him, the more I become like Him. The more I become like Him, the more His reality becomes my reality. Then I become what Ephesians 4:13 calls, **"a perfect man of full stature."**

The Power of Agreement

As I mentioned earlier, most of us are walking in a reality base on our experiences.

In the process of growing up, a child goes through various stages of development. If those involved with the raising of the child can shield him or her from as many negative experiences as possible, the child has a chance of growing and becoming a mentally and emotionally healthy person. They're able to function successfully in society. Their reality has been developed in a safe, nurturing, and loving environment. They learn to be more outgoing, sociable, and creative. They're open to learning new things and willing to explore and become more adventurous. They're always upbeat and see challenges as opportunities rather than obstacles. They're encouraging and uplifting. They see the glass half full rather than half empty. This type of environment causes a child to view the world in a healthy way.

But if a child is exposed to negative experiences at an early age, the child's normal development is brought to a halt because of the trauma they have or are experiencing. What happens then is at the point of the trauma, if the child is not properly cared for mentally and emotionally, they move from what is known as the developmental stage to survival. They begin to live a life of fear, anxiety, and the inability to trust. They may grow up angry, depressed, and introverted. They're unable to have healthy relationships. They're unable to give or receive love. Their self-worth and esteem is nonexistent. They feel inadequate and unstable. Rejection and betrayal runs deep emotionally. And from this they become performance based and if they don't perform well, they feel like failures. They're unable to excel in school and they're quick to give up on or not even try new things. They give up on others and even themselves.

They resort to violence and maybe a life of crime. And they have no respect for authority. We see this reality everywhere. The first reality is more open to hear and receive the good news of Jesus' love than the second reality. This is because their negative experiences are few and far between. And they're always open to new experiences whereas the second is not. This is because they're living in a quagmire of hurt, pain, anger, hopelessness, and fear. They're not quick to trust anybody. Not even God.

Both of these realities started with one common foundation, agreement. Both of them came into agreement with their experiences and those experiences created their prospective realities.

You might say they had no choice. They were children. Yes, you're right. They were children when their individual experience began. But when they reach teenage or even adulthood, they came into the ability to choose.

The most power gift the Lord gave to mankind is the power to choose. Choice is power. Even Almighty God Himself can be unable to move by the choices we make.

Yea, they turned back and tempted God, and
limited the Holy One of Israel
Psalm 78:41

Each of us possesses the power to choose. We can choose to do good or evil. We can remain in a dysfunctional lifestyle or make the choice to change.

Here's an example. You have 2 young men living in a neighborhood filled with violence, drug use and abuse, and all sorts of depravation, discouragement, and hopelessness. They both go to the same school. All sorts of temptations and peer pressure surround them both.

The Power of Agreement

They're both being raised by just one parent because the other parent was killed in random violence on the very streets they live. And neighborhood gangs approach them both on various occasions to join them.

Now here's where agreement through choice begins to shape their reality; one of the 2 gives in to the ways and pressures of the society in which he lives. He's living in pain and anger because of the loss of his parent. He begins to take drugs. His grades drop dramatically and he becomes disruptive in school; He stays out late. He's disobedient to his parent. He takes on a violent nature and begins to get into fights. He starts to steal. And finally, he joins the local gang and begins a life of crime. He's given up on people, life, and even himself.

The other one however is different. He sets goals for his future. He learns and matures from the death of his parent. He studies hard in school and has the highest grade point average in his class. After school he goes to his part-time job and works hard for his employer. He brings home his pay, gives his parent some money for assistance and he helps out around the home. He graduates from High school as valedictorian with the highest grade point average in his entire graduating class and receives an academic scholarship. He goes to college, receives his bachelors degree. Then goes to undergraduate school and obtains his master. And finally goes on to get His Doctorate. He becomes a best selling author, a great public speaker, consultant, counselor, and mentor. He gets married and has 2 children and moves into a beautiful home. He goes back to the old neighborhood and brings his parent out and buys them a nice home and a car just because he loves them and appreciates the sacrifices they made for him. And he lives a prosperous and fruitful life, loved and admired by many.

Two young men, same neighborhood, same circumstance, same challenges, same pressures, same depravations, and possess the same perspectives. But both make 2 different decisions and births 2 different realities. And although these were examples, this scenario is real in every culture in our world.

Many in the body of Christ and all of humanity are living from perspective rather than reality. What do I mean by this? As I mentioned earlier, the word reality deals with what is real, true, actual, and authentic. But perspective deals with a point of view, a perception, or an outlook. Perspective is created out of experience and if those experiences are negative, they can distort ones reality. For example, when a woman is raped she has suffered a major trauma. Not only is her body violated, but her emotions and psyche has been violated. And even though the reality of that experience is over for months and even years, unless the woman receives some form of mental and emotional therapy, the woman will see life, more specifically, men, from the perspective of her experience. And when a man who is safe comes along, he may touch her or even say something that triggers her memories of the experience and cause her to lash out or even reject the man altogether. It's not that the man has done anything wrong. It's the fact that the woman is still living in the experience when the reality is that it's over.

God meant for us to always walk in the reality of who we are in Him. He desires us to walk in the reality of His plan for all of humanity. But because of sin, we live from perspective rather than reality. God has to literally war with our thinking to get us to "realize" who we are in Him. He has to convince us through His word and experiencing His presence that how we see ourselves is contrary to how He's created us. The reality is we are new creatures in Christ.

The Power of Agreement

Therefore if any man be in Christ, he is a new
creature: old things are passed away; behold,
all things are become new
II Corinthians 5:17

The problem is many of God's people still walk from the perspective of the old man rather than the reality of the new man created in God through Jesus Christ. Many of us still believe that we're always going to be the way we are and all we can do is hold on until Christ returns and then we'll become like Him. But the reality is He has commanded us to take on the character and nature of Christ through the indwelling operation of the Holy Spirit and retake dominion of the earth by coming into the reality and fulfillment of our purpose, to walk in the power and demonstration of the Holy Spirit, and living according to the word of God.

And I, brethren, when I came to you, came not
with excellency of speech or of wisdom,
declaring unto you the testimony of God. For I
determined not to know any thing among you,
save Jesus Christ, and him crucified. And I was
with you in weakness, and in fear, and in much
trembling. And my speech and my preaching
was not with enticing words of man's wisdom,
but in demonstration of the Spirit and of power:
That your faith should not stand in the wisdom
of men, but in the power of God
I Corinthians 2:1-5

Nay, in all these things we are more than
conquerors through him that loved us
Romans 8:37

30

Blessed is the man that walketh not in the counsel of the ungodly, nor standeth in the way of sinners, nor sitteth in the seat of the scornful. But his delight is in the law of the LORD; and in his law doth he meditate day and night. And he shall be like a tree planted by the rivers of water, that bringeth forth his fruit in his season; his leaf also shall not wither; and whatsoever he doeth shall prosper
Psalm 1:1-3

Before Adam rebelled against God, he walked in the reality of who he was in God and his position as God's representative in the earth. He lived in a reality filled with the unlimited riches of creation and the unlimited glory of God's presence. His reality was totally God-centered and God-focused. But when he sinned, his eyes were opened. He didn't take on a new reality but he took on a new perspective. The reality of who he was didn't change, but his perspective of who he was change. He was no longer totally conscious of the presence of God. He was now totally conscious of self. In other words, his perspective took control of his reality and opened the door to be totally self-centered, influenced and controlled by the flesh and the devil. And through this experience we became separated from God.

But if our gospel be hid, it is hid to them that are lost: In whom the god of this world hath blinded the minds of them which believe not, lest the light of the glorious gospel of Christ, who is the image of God, should shine unto them
II Corinthians 4:3,4

The Power of Agreement

But we thank God that He came in the form of Jesus Christ and presented us with a new perspective which would bring us back into the proper reality of our place in God. All we need do is come into agreement with it and allow the inward working of the Holy Spirit to make it so (Ephesians 3:14-19).
We are spiritual beings. This reality has never changed. Our souls and bodies are instruments created by God for us to function here in the earth. We are designed to function from the reality of the spirit. Not from the perspective of the world. This is why we war between reality and perspective. And whichever controls us causes us to function from that paradigm of though.

For they that are after the flesh do mind the
things of the flesh; but they that are after the
Spirit the things of the Spirit
Romans 8:5

It is time for us to come into agreement with the reality of God and His original plan for mankind. As long as we live in harmony with the world's perspective, we will always live beneath our privileges of being the kings, priests, and heirs of God. But when you and I come into agreement with who we are in God and forsake everything that is opposed to this reality, we can truly live as overcomers, more than conquerors, and Christ can truly be the first born among many brethren.

For whom he did foreknow, he also did
predestinate to be conformed to the image of
his Son, that he might be the firstborn among
many brethren
Romans 8:29

32

Chapter 4
Agreement with our Past

No matter how hard many of us try to move forward in our lives, the past always seems to be present. Memories of days long since gone by seem to flow endlessly through our minds. Some memories we've been able to learn from. Some have made us more mature, wiser, prosperous and successful. And some we've been able to put behind us and look forward to bigger and better things. But there are some that we never seem to forget. They are so entrenched in our psyche we just can't seem to get past them. Whether positive or negative, people, places, or things, these memories are always present. And some memories are so vivid and have impacted us so deeply they can literally dictate our present and even our future.

We have memories we don't want to let go of, which speak of wonderful times, filling us with joy, laughter, and peace, which encourages and strengthens us.

This I recall to my mind, therefore have I hope
Lamentations 3:16

But there are some memories that are so traumatic they haunt us continually. They torment us to such a degree they affect us mentally, emotionally, and physically. We're unable to develop healthy relationships, achieve goals and dreams, move up the corporate ladder, and even come into a deeper relationship with our Lord.

Even when I remember, I am troubled and
afraid; horror and trembling take hold of my
flesh
Job 21:6
The Amplified Version

The Power of Agreement

These types of memories literally cripple us. These memories imprison us mentally. They even force some of us to altar our lives to extremes. There are people who refuse to pursue a meaningful relationship with the opposite sex because of the pain of a past relationship. Some have even turned to homosexuality because past relationships with the opposite sex failed. Some are afraid to go outside their homes because of a past experience. So become isolated because of feelings of inadequacy developed from past situations. The past can be so powerful it can cause us to settle for things we know we shouldn't because we've become so overly cautious and just plan afraid of what the outcome would be because the memories of past experiences says *"if you do this, it might happen again."*

In the last chapter I spoke about how our perspective is affected by our experiences. And those perspectives, left unchecked, can control our reality. It is an unhealed perspective that constantly rewinds the tapes of past negative experiences. And these past experiences control our ability to make decision which can improve, hinder, or destroy our ministry, life and the life of the next generation.

God has so many things in store for His people. There are blessings and promises that await each of us. And God wishes to reveal them to us that we may obtain them.

But as it is written, Eye hath not seen, nor ear heard, neither have entered into the heart of man, the things which God hath prepared for them that love him. But God hath revealed them unto us by his Spirit: for the Spirit searcheth all things, yea, the deep things of God
I Corinthians 2:9,10

Grace and peace be multiplied unto you
through the knowledge of God, and of Jesus
our Lord, According as his divine power hath
given unto us all things that pertain unto life
and godliness, through the knowledge of him
that hath called us to glory and virtue
II Peter 1:2,3

With all that God has prepared for us, the one promise I wish to focus on is the promise of being conformed to His image and likeness.

For whom he did foreknow, he also did
predestinate to be conformed to the image of
his Son, that he might be the firstborn among
many brethren
Romans 8:29

In order for us to come into the reality of His image and likeness we must first divorce ourselves from the past.

Remember ye not the former things, neither
consider the things of old
Isaiah 43:18

There is absolutely no way we can come into the fullness of God and still remain a prisoner of the past. One has to be sacrificed if the other is going to exist.

The root cause of a believer's in ability to walk into the reality of the promises of God is fear. Fear is probably the one key element that prevents the believer from realizing the deeper things of God. The first thing Adam said to God after he sinned was, ***"I heard thy voice and I was afraid."***

The Power of Agreement

> *And they heard the voice of the LORD God*
> *walking in the garden in the cool of the day:*
> *and the man and his wife hid themselves from*
> *the presence of the LORD God amongst the*
> *trees of the garden. And the LORD God called*
> *unto the man, and said* unto him, Where art
> thou? And he said, I *heard thy voice in the*
> *garden, and I was afraid*, because I was naked;
> and I hid myself
> *Genesis 3:8-10*

You may ask yourself, "fear of what?" There are many forms of fear humans struggle with. But I believe in this case there is 2 forms of fear that can and do immobilize many believers. The first is **fear of the unknown** and the second is **fear of being vulnerable or exposed**.

The fear of the unknown

The word unknown is defined as, *not known; not within the range of one's knowledge, experience, or understanding; strange; unfamiliar; not discovered, explored, identified, or ascertained.*

> *But as it is written, Eye hath not seen, nor ear*
> *heard, neither have entered into the heart of*
> *man, the things which God hath prepared for*
> *them that love him*
> *I Corinthians 2:9*

In today's society, mankind lives by what I call **sense knowledge**. This is knowledge received and processed by way of the 5 senses-sight, sound, taste, smell, and touch.

Those led by these 5 senses in essence must have some form of physical evidence before they make any type of decision to pursue what they've come to desire. But in the kingdom of God, we're called to go forward to obtain what God has promised not on the basis of sense knowledge but on the basis of faith and His word. This is because God reveals the promise but He doesn't reveal the journey.

> *So then faith cometh by hearing, and hearing by the word of God...By faith Abraham, when he was called to go out into a place which he should after receive for an inheritance, obeyed; and he went out, **not knowing whither he went***
> *Romans 10:17; Hebrews 11:8*

This is where the fear of the unknown manifests because we don't know how to get there. Not knowing how to get there literally strips us of control and self-sufficiency and compels us to rely completely on God.

> *Trust in the LORD with all thine heart; and lean not unto thine own understanding. In all thy ways acknowledge him, and he shall direct thy paths*
> *Proverbs 3:5,6*

The definition of faith is **the assent of the mind or understanding to the truth of what God has revealed.** It's a conviction that what God has promised He will do. It is a willingness to go through the process God requires to come into the reality of His promise with only His word as evidence that it exist and that I will obtain it because He promised.

The Power of Agreement

Faith requires us to ignore past experiences and believe God in spite of it all.

Abraham, a man raised in a society filled with pagan religious and cultural practices for 75 years, a man who has strong family ties and devotion to his people, and is committed to the care of his family, hears a word from a God He's never seen, heard, or known before, that He would give him a land for an inheritance and make Him a great nation when he and his wife Sarah are childless and past child baring age. He has everything he's ever known and loved before him, but he is compelled by the promise to obey this unknown God's will even when everything around him in a physical sense points to the impossibility of this ever happening. And along with this he has no idea where this land of promise is, nor how far he has to travel to get there.

It is a frightful thing to step out on just a word even when it is coming from a faithful, loving, promise-keeping God. To look at everything, which says *"no"* and still move forward on the word of God which says *"yes"* requires faith to do this. But it also requires a strength to forget because in the process of looking forward to our future our past negative experiences will scream in opposition. But we must break free from the stronghold of our negative past in order to come into what God has for us and the ability to forget is a powerful weapon that can break us free into our destiny.

Brethren, I count not myself to have apprehended: but this one thing I do, ***forgetting those things which are behind, and reaching forth unto those things which are before****, I press toward the mark for the prize of the high calling of God in Christ Jesus Philippians 3:13,14*

The fear of being vulnerable or exposed

*And they heard the voice of the LORD God
walking in the garden in the cool of the day:
and Adam and his wife hid themselves from
the presence of the LORD God amongst the
trees of the garden. And the LORD God called
unto Adam, and said unto him, Where art
thou? And he said, **I heard thy voice in the
garden, and I was afraid, because I was
naked; and I hid myself***
Genesis 3:8-10

The words vulnerable and expose are being used together because one cannot be vulnerable without exposing one's self. And one cannot expose one's self without first making a decision to become vulnerable.

The word expose is defined as, *To subject or allow to be subjected to an action, influence, or condition; to disclose to view as by removing a cover.*

Being vulnerable or exposing one's self is, in my estimation, at the top of the list of things we fear most. It takes a great deal of strength and courage to reveal one's heart and mind without wondering whether the person we're bearing our soul to (excluding God) is going to put a knife though it mainly because it has happened before or we know those who have experienced it and to see the trauma they are coping with compels us to put our walls up for protection. In today's society, I don't think there's anyone over the age of 2 or 3 that has not experienced some type of trauma that has taught us to be protective of ourselves.

We encounter people on a daily basis that have been traumatized.

The Power of Agreement

People walking in the present, but living in the past. And unfortunately, many of these people (you may be one of them) have yet to fully recover from those past experiences.

We've been taught by experience and people not to trust so easily. We've been advised by people not to give our confidence, trust, or even our hearts to so easily. We know people just by mere observation, that they have been deeply wounded and they have yet to recover. And some of those wounds go back as far as their childhood.

We are exposed to the pain and anger of those we're acquainted with or are close to because as they speak with us they always seem to end up talking about their painful experience. As you attempt to offer an optimistic alternative they in many ways become defensive and even protective of their trauma. Or as we share with them, something we may say that has absolutely nothing to do with their situation will produce a negative emotional response that reveals the pain, frustration, and anger rooted in their past experience.

These are people whom remain in a perpetual state of agreement with their past. Although the experience is over, they continue to rehearse the experience over and over in their minds, making it as though the experience is still taking place. This makes it difficult for God to release healing into the wounded places of our hearts because we can't or we refuse to let go. We become unable or even unwilling to yield ourselves to potentially healthy relationships because we won't let go of the unhealthy relationships either literally or psychologically. And it gets so bad that even Almighty God is unable to impart the solution because we choose to remain in agreement with the problem.

Once a week I conduct bible study at the county prison. Some of the inmates there are facing short terms and some are facing long terms, and some are even facing life.

In the time I spend with them I see they're good men and sincere about their walk with the Lord. They study the word and some of them know the word better than I do.

And as they share their hearts I can see that many of them if not all of them have experienced some major trauma in their life and because of this it placed them on a path of destruction and to ultimately be where they are now.

But my greatest challenge with my brothers in prison is convincing them their lives are not over. They still have a future and a purpose in God. And they can experience the joy, peace, love and the healing power of the Holy Spirit.

But when you're living in a closed environment with so many men in the same situation and 90% of all discussion is about your past and what you're about to face in court, it can be very difficult to focus on your future in God when all you see is the potential for more jail time as a result of your past.

This same situation is evident in the lives of people who're not in a physical prison but they're in a mental and emotional one. They're imprisoned by the traumas of their experience and the warden is the enemy which continues to play the memories of those experiences over and over in their minds, making them feel they can never be free from they're past and this is the way it will always be. They'll never be able to trust, they'll never be able to love, and they will never be able to have a life filled with joy and peace.

For the enemy hath persecuted my soul; he hath smitten my life down to the ground; he hath made me to dwell in darkness, as those that have been long dead. Therefore is my spirit overwhelmed within me; my heart within me is desolate
Psalm 143:3,4

41

The Power of Agreement

Breaking free from the darkness of our past

But even though our past seems to be always haunting us, we can overcome it by making the choice to release it. Some of us will experience some immediate breakthroughs. But for some of us it will take time, effort, and perseverance to break free from that which as tormented us for so many years. Here are some ways we can use to set us free. They've worked for me and I believe they'll work for you.

The first one is **confession**. Confession is defined as, **the disburdening of the conscience.** *"Confession is the doorway to healing and deliverance."* As we open up and share our experiences with someone we can be vulnerable with and expose ourselves to, we open the door to God, allowing Him access to the pain and memories of our experience. There He begins to operate on us, bringing us into a new and refreshing reality of His life, His love, and His faithfulness.

Confess your faults one to another, and pray
one for another, that ye may be healed
James 5:16a

The next one is **forgiveness**. Forgiveness is defined as, **the pardon of an offender of sin or of injuries by which he is considered and treated as not guilty.** This is a very important point and yet it can be very difficult for us who have been deeply wounded, especially by those in our family and those close to us because of the deep feelings of betrayal that comes with the offense. This must be dealt with if healing is going to be released from God to us because if we don't forgive we can't be forgiven (Mark 11:25,26).

Forgiveness is especially important for 2 reasons. One, unforgiveness causes a separation in our relationship between God and us. It hinders our prayer-life and diminishes our sensitivity to God-the Holy Spirit, and opens the door to the presence and influence of the enemy.

God is a loving and forgiving God. That's His nature. That's why He sent Lord Jesus to die for us to set up the plan by which we can receive forgiveness through Christ and be brought back into right relationship with Him and God commands us to be as forgiving as He is-no exceptions.

In my life one my greatest challenge is receiving my healing through forgiving my stepfather. I never knew my biological father although I saw pictures of him and spoke with him once on the phone when I was about 12 years old. My stepfather, whom I acknowledge as my father because he's been in my life since I was about 2 or 3 years old, was an alcoholic and very verbally, mentally, emotionally and sometimes physically abusive to me. He would call me things like stupid, dumb, good for nothing, and told me I'd never to amount to anything. He would get drunk and do some really horrible things to me. And then wake up the next morning asking for forgiveness. He would tell my mother he was taking me fishing (which was something I loved) and pick up one of his friends and then go to the bar and stay there with his friend drinking for hours, leaving me in the car. Needless to say we never went fishing. I realized after a few of these experiences that he was just using me to get out of the house to go and drink. His apologies got to the point that I didn't want to hear them anymore. Now there were some good times. But they were heavily out-weighed by the bad.

As I got older I became more and more resentful towards him. And soon my resentment towards him graduated to anger an even hatred.

43

The Power of Agreement

I'm 43 years old now and I am still dealing with dysfunctions stemming from many of the things he did to me growing up. God has healed me from some of those experiences and I praise and thank Him for it. But now He's requiring of me something deeper in order to receive the rest of my healing and that's spending time with my father.

Now some you may think that's not so trying. But you ask someone you know who has been deeply hurt by a relative or any person, when their pain has not been resolved, how difficult it is to be around that person knowing what they have done to them. It is mentally hard and emotionally trying. But while I'm there, I can sense in the midst of our time together, God working humility, love, and healing in me, and as I submit to His will and God heals me it is no longer as difficult as it use to be.

Now I love my father more than I have in the past. But I must confess, it still takes allot for me to stay there but it's getting easier to stay there as well. But I know that as I continue to go and spend time with him, and I confess my forgiveness towards him (by my actions), God is going to perfect that which concerns me and I will be a better man, a better man of God, and a better father.

Surprisingly enough there are many of us who love and serve God who are going through the same process. Confession and forgiveness is a very power and challenging aspect of eliminating past negative experiences from tormenting and even hindering us from coming into our destiny. But if we continue to trust God He will keep His promise and bring us through.

But he knoweth the way that I take: when he
hath tried me, I shall come forth as gold
Job 23:10
44

The second reason is unforgiveness, depending on the depth of the hurt, if left unchecked, can lead to mental, emotional, physical deterioration, and even death.

When I gave my life to Christ in September of 1993, I began attending a church where I met a woman of God through the pastor's son, who became my mentor and who is now my pastor. She introduced me to a couple who had been there since the church's inception. As my mentor and I spent time with them, and I began to get to know them, I began to see that the husband was verbally abusive to his wife and kids. It reminded me of some of what happened to me growing up.

As my mentor and I spent more time with the couple to assist them through some difficult times they were having, the husband began to share with me some things he had been through in the church. I shared with my mentor what he shared with me. And she, having known them much long than I had, began to fill in the blanks.

It seemed that this man of God was deeply hurt in the church. For reasons unknown to me he was past over when certain high-ranking positions became open.

Because of this he became very distraught, angry, and bitter. He began to go to school and accumulate various degrees, including his doctorate of divinity to prove to the people he was somebody. But they still didn't acknowledge him.

As a result of internalizing his anger and bitterness, his health began to deteriorate. He developed diabetes, his kidneys began to fail and he had to have dialysis done at least once a week. And to make matters worst, he ended up with cancer and with a year or two, he died. You might think after he passed away that it was all over. But that's not the end of this tragic story.

The Power of Agreement

While he was alive, I mentioned he was verbally, mentally, and emotionally abusive towards his wife and kids. His wife was so overwhelmed with stress, depression, and fear, she began having heart attacks. His kids didn't want to have anything to do with him. And after his death, the children didn't want to have anything to do with church and the wife, 6 months after the death of her husband, died herself from heart failure. Now ask yourself, ***"is it really worth holding on to that pain and anger?"***

And the 3rd and final one is prayer and the presence of God.

> *The effectual fervent prayer of the righteous*
> *man availeth much… In thy presence is fulness*
> *of joy; at thy right hand there are pleasures*
> *forevermore*
> *James 5:16b; Psalm 16:11b*

When we enter into sincere yielded Spirit-led prayer, we enter into the presence of God. As we're in the midst of prayer, our souls are open to flow of the Holy Spirit and through prayer He can begin to minister to the broken places our hearts.

Prayer doesn't just deal with the object of our prayer; it also deals with the person being used in prayer.

> *Now the Lord is that Spirit: and where the Spirit*
> *of the Lord is, there is liberty*
> *II Corinthians 3:17*

As we release God into the dark places of our lives we can be set free from all that bind us so we can look forward to new and awesome things God has in store for us.

Chapter 5
Agreement and our Destiny

But arise and stand upon your feet; for I have
appeared to you for this purpose, that I might
appoint you to serve as [My] minister and to
bear witness both to what you have seen of Me
and to that in which I will appear to you,
Choosing you out [selecting you for Myself]
and delivering you from among this [Jewish]
people and the Gentiles to whom I am sending
you to open their eyes that they may turn from
darkness to light and from the power of satan
to God, so that they may thus receive
forgiveness and release from their sins and a
place and portion among those who are
consecrated and purified by faith in Me
Acts 26:16-18
The Amplified Version

I cannot overemphasize how important it is for us to
come into agreement with our destiny. The word destiny isn't
found in the bible. But the entire bible speaks of destiny and
the importance of its fulfillment. Every person that has or will
walk this earth is here by the sovereign will of God for one
reason and one reason only, and that reason is destiny.

Before I formed thee in the belly I knew thee;
and before thou camest forth out of the womb I
sanctified thee, and I ordained thee...
Jeremiah 1:5

Destiny is the most fulfilling aspect of one's life
because we come into divine alignment with the universal
will of God and eternal encounters with the Lord of glory.

47

The Power of Agreement

Destiny is defined as, **a fixed order of things established by a divine decree**.

> ...for I am God, and there is none else; I am God, and there is none like me, Declaring the end from the beginning, and from ancient times the things that are not yet done, saying, My counsel shall stand, and I will do all my pleasure
> Isaiah 46:9,10

> For I know that thoughts and plans that I have for you, says the Lord, thoughts and plans for welfare and peace and not for evil, to give you hope in our final outcome
> Jeremiah 29:11
> The Amplified Version

It was destiny that compelled God to create the heavens and the earth. It was destiny that moved God to create man. It was destiny that called the children of Israel out of Egypt to bring them into the promise land. It was destiny that sent Lord Jesus to die on the cross to redeem man back to God. And it was destiny that caused Christ to send the Holy Spirit to birth the church to be His corporate body to manifest His character and nature to the world.

Only God can reveal our true destiny for it is He that established our destiny and created us for that very purpose.

We can succeed in so many areas of life outside of our God-ordained destiny. We can receive an abundance of accolades and make millions of dollars outside of destiny. We can have a wonderful job and a great marriage outside of destiny.

We can raise wonderful children, and develop fantastic friendships outside of destiny. We can possess cars, houses, land, and travel around the world outside of destiny. But if we're not pursuing and fulfilling our God-ordained destiny we possess nothing nor have we accomplished anything in life, let alone for God.

> *Because thou sayest, I am rich, and increased with goods, and have need of nothing; and knowest not that thou art wretched, and miserable, and poor, and blind, and naked*
> *Revelation 3:17*

Destiny must be our number one priority. If destiny isn't our focus we are susceptible to manipulation and deception by man's opinion and the influence of the enemy. A life without destiny is a life filled with confusion, frustration, fear, and uncertainty. There's an old saying which fittingly applies which is, *"if you don't know where you're going any road will take you there."*

When we are operating in our divine destiny we walk in a level of faith and confidence that is unshakable. It gives us a boldness that causes us to go wherever God commands and releases His power in any and every forum He desires. When we're walking in our destiny we can pray with boldness because we know He hears us because we're operating in His perfect and ordained will. When we're operating in the plan of God we can move in the authority God says we have in His Son. We can declare to the enemy and all that oppose the sovereign will of God to come subject in the name of Jesus when we're in the will of God's plan for our lives and the kingdom. And He assures us that if we ask anything according to His will He hears us.

49

The Power of Agreement

Let me give you some examples of destiny.

Noah's destiny was to build an ark to save his family and become the heir of a new world.

> *By faith Noah, being warned of God of things not seen as yet, moved with fear, prepared an ark to the saving of his house; by the which he condemned the world, and became heir of the righteousness which is by faith*
> *Hebrews 11:7*

Abraham's destiny was to come out of a pagan lifestyle culture and become the father of many nations

> *Now the LORD had said unto Abram, Get thee out of thy country, and from thy kindred, and from thy father's house, unto a land that I will show thee: And I will make of thee a great nation, and I will bless thee, and make thy name great; and thou shalt*
> *be a blessing*
> *Genesis 12:1,2*

Joseph's destiny was to be a savior to Israel and the world.

> *And God sent me before you to preserve you a posterity in the earth, and to save your lives by a great deliverance. So now it was not you that sent me hither, but God: and he hath made me a father to Pharaoh, and lord of all his house, and a ruler throughout all the land of Egypt*
> *Genesis 45:7,8*

Joshua was destined to succeed Moses and lead the children of Israel into the land God promised them to possess it for an inheritance.

> And the LORD said unto Moses, Behold, thy days approach that thou must die: call Joshua, and present yourselves in the tabernacle of the congregation, that I may give him a charge. And Moses and Joshua went, and presented themselves in the tabernacle of the congregation...And he gave Joshua the son of Nun a charge, and said, Be strong and of a good courage: for thou shalt bring the children of Israel into the land which I swore unto them: and I will be with thee
> Deuteronomy 31:14,23

When we come into agreement with our destiny we release the resources and provision God has promised us to fulfill His will. There is nothing withheld from us when we go forth in God and perform that which we're commissioned to.

> For the LORD God is a sun and shield: the LORD will give grace and glory: no good thing will he withhold from them that walk uprightly
> Psalm 84:11

When we come into agreement with our destiny we come under the divine protection of God. When we go forth and do the will of God His glory overshadows us and angels which have been given charge over us are standing at the ready to do battle with the kingdom of darkness that would oppose those of us who strive to fulfill our mission in Christ.

The Power of Agreement

*The God of my rock; in him will I trust: he is my
shield, and the horn of my salvation, my high
tower, and my refuge, my savior; thou savest
me from violence*
II Samuel 22:3

With destiny comes a process. With destiny comes
brokenness, pruning, purging, purifying, and cleansing.

*But he knoweth the way that I take: when he
hath tried me, I shall come forth as gold*
Job 23:10

In his book, *Spiritual Leadership*, J. Oswald Sanders
shares a surreal poem of God taking His chosen through
before presenting them to the world for His divine purpose:

When God wants to drill a man, and thrill and
man and skill a man, When God wants to mold
man to play the noblest part; When He yearns
with all His heart to create so great and bold a
man that all the world shall be amazed, Watch
His methods, watch His way! How He
ruthlessly perfects Whom He royally elects!
How He hammers him and hurts him, and with
mighty blows converts him, into trial shapes of
clay which only God understands; while his
tortured heart is crying and he lifts beseeching
hands! How He bends but never breaks when
his good he undertakes; How He uses whom
He chooses and with every purpose fuses him;
But every act includes him to try His splendor
out-God knows what He's about

52

Agreement with our Destiny

With destiny also comes adversity. The one thing, next to salvation, the enemy doesn't want a person to realize is their destiny. He will do everything he can to thwart a man or woman from coming into the reality of their God ordained purpose. This is why he doesn't wait until we're saved to destroy us. He comes after us from the moment of our birth.

> *And when they were departed, behold, the angel of the Lord appeareth to Joseph in a dream, saying, Arise, and take the young child and his mother, and flee into Egypt, and be thou there until I bring thee word: for Herod will seek the young child to destroy him. ..Then Herod, when he saw that he was mocked of the wise men, was exceeding wroth, and sent forth, and slew all the children that were in Bethlehem, and in all the coasts thereof, from two years old and under, according to the time which he had diligently inquired of the wise men*
> *Matthew 2:13,16*

The Lord is saying:

For even as satan attempted to kill Moses at his birth by killing the children of his generation because of his destiny, and even as he attempted to kill My Son at His birth by killing all of the male children of His generation because of his destiny, the enemy is going throughout the land killing my children once again because he knows there is a great birth taking place in the earth.

53

The Power of Agreement

He knows that a great move of My Spirit being birthed into the earth and he's attempting to kill as many of my children as he can to prevent them from being used for my glory to bring his kingdom down. But what he doesn't know is that I will send those whom he has slain back to the earth for my glory. I will rebirth them into the earth and show them openly to the king of darkness and declare unto him, "I AM THE RESURRECTION AND THE LIFE." though you slay my chosen I will raise them up again to do all my pleasure in the earth. I will rebirth my children into the earth for there is a great work that I have for them to accomplish in the earth before the return of My Son. Says the Lord of Host.

Although the enemy uses adversity to discourage and bewilder us, God uses adversity to train and develop us. He uses the enemy's plans against him to produce a strong, powerful, and united army, walking in humility, love, and compassion. We rise up from the struggles and obstacles of the enemy, possessing the ability to persevere and overcome anything he puts before us. Out of adversity we're trained and equipped in the fruit and gifts of the Spirit that we might combat the enemy and bring his kingdom down.

He disappointeth the devices of the crafty, so that their hands cannot perform their enterprise. He taketh the wise in their own craftiness: and the counsel of the froward is carried headlong
Job 5:12,13

But true destiny in God is really becoming who we are in Him and then what we do for Him. Sometimes we can get so caught up in doing for God we forget that the heart of our destiny is becoming like God.

And God said, Let us make man in our image, after our likeness...For whom he did foreknow, he also did predestinate to be conformed to the image of his Son, that he might be the firstborn among many brethren
Genesis 1:26a; Romans 8:29

It is our destiny to walk in the image and likeness of Lord Jesus. This has been the glorious plan of God from the very beginning. This was the reason the Father sent Christ to suffer, die, and rise from the grave in order to reposition us to fulfill God's original plan of walking in His image and likeness and reestablish our divine fellowship with Him.

The purpose of the great commission is not just to preach the gospel and demonstrate the power to God. Those are the instruments designed by God. The purpose of the great commission is for us to lead souls back to God through Christ so they may become who they were destined to be which is the image and likeness of God in Christ.

*For whom he did foreknow, **he also did predestinate to be conformed to the image of his Son**, that he might be the firstborn among many brethren*
Romans 8:29

If we don't come into the reality of the image and likeness of God we're not fulfilling the totality of our destiny.

55

The Power of Agreement

It's good we're building ministries, preaching and teaching the word, saving souls, prospering, building business, and giving to the poor. It's good we're clothing the naked, laying hands on the sick and seeing them recover. It's good we're casting out devils. It's good we're praying and interceding, and building Christian school. But if we don't allow the Holy Spirit to conform us to the full image of Christ we're coming short of His divine plan.

We cannot allow reasoning, doctrinal theology, denominational, religious, traditional beliefs and just plan insecurity to be so predominant in our lives and ministries that we come short of fulfilling the Father's plan for His creation.

This desire of the Father's heart is evident in the prayer Paul prayed for the Ephesian church.

> *For this reason [seeing the greatness of this plan by which you are built together in Christ], I bow my knees before the Father of our Lord Jesus Christ, For Whom every family in heaven and on earth is named [that Father from Whom all fatherhood takes its title and derives its name]. May He grant you out of the rich treasury of His glory to be strengthened and reinforced with mighty power in the inner man by the [Holy] Spirit [Himself indwelling your innermost being and personality]. May Christ through your faith [actually] dwell (settle down, abide, make His permanent home) in your hearts! May you be rooted deep in love and founded securely on love, That you may have the power and be strong to apprehend and grasp with all the saints [God's devoted people,*

*the experience of that love] what is the breadth
and length and height and depth [of it]; [that
you may really come] to know [practically,
through experience for yourselves] the love of
Christ, which far surpasses mere knowledge
[without experience]; that you may be filled
[through all your being] unto all the fullness of
God [may have the richest measure of the
divine Presence, and become and body wholly
filled and flooded with God Himself]!
Ephesians 3:14-19
The Amplified Version*

This is the will of God concerning us. God is saying to us in these last days, we will see men and women, boys and girls, young and old, rich and pour, which have given themselves over completely to the will of God, experience the greatest manifestation of the character and nature of God that can only be compared with Lord Jesus Himself when He walked the earth. We're going to see that man-child that Ephesians 4:13 and Revelation 12:1,2,5 speaks of.

We will hear them utter those same powerful and yet humble words Lord Jesus expressed as He explained to the religious people of His day that He came, in agreement with the Father, controlled and influenced by Him alone, to fulfill, not His will, but the will of His heavenly Father.

*Verily, verily, I say unto you, The Son can do
nothing of himself, but what he seeth the
Father do: for what things soever he doeth,
these also doeth the Son likewise...I and my
Father are one
John 5:19; John 10:30*

The Power of Agreement

We're going to see Christ walking the earth once again in fullness in the lives of His chosen people through the Holy Spirit to bring His bride to full maturity and to position us for Christ's literal return. There will be signs, wonders, and miracles that we've never seen before. The love of God will emanate from His people like never before. We will see men and women, filled with all the fullness of God going into places that the religious and traditional church has called "off limits" and demonstrate the love and power of God to a dying people and through this great demonstration of the Spirit we will draw multiplied millions into the kingdom for Christ and cause all that are willing and obedient to enter into the experiential knowledge of walking in the fullness of God for themselves. Get ready! It's destined to happen! Will you be a part of it?

But I say, walk and live [habitually] in the [Holy] Spirit [responsive to and controlled and guided by the Spirit]; then you will certainly not gratify the cravings and desires of the flesh (of human nature without God)... If we live by the [Holy] Spirit, let us also walk by the Spirit. [If by the Holy Spirit we have our life in God, let us go forward walking in line, our conduct controlled by the Spirit.]
Galatians 5:16,25
The Amplified Version

Chapter 6
Generational Agreements

And the LORD said, Shall I hide from Abraham
that thing which I do…For I know him, that he
will command his children and his household
after him, and they shall keep the way of the
LORD, to do justice and judgment; that the
LORD may bring upon Abraham that which he
hath spoken of him
Genesis 18:17,19

As I read the word of God, I've come to realize that of all the things God is passionate about, God is most passionate about family. He instituted the family structure because not only is God love, He's a God that loves family. Before the foundations of the world, the desire for family was the motivation of God. He, God, didn't birth the church to be some religious, ritualistic, divided, money driven, idolatrous organization; but He birth the church to be a family of many nations of people called to be united together as one loving, joyous, powerful organism; created to function as a single unit called the family of God (Jeremiah 3:14).

God has been and is still all about family. The reason He created man was to enjoy the pleasures of Fatherhood and to see generations of children, created in His image and likeness, populate the earth and honor Him as their Father and Jesus as their elder brother (Romans 8:29).

The reason He created the heavens and the earth, the sun and moon, the stars and planets, the oceans and seas, and all plant and animal life was so He and His family can have a place to meet, commune and enjoy one another.

The Lord created man to pass on His character, nature, knowledge, love, wisdom, and authority to the next generation to walk in dominion over all of creation.

59

The Power of Agreement

And God said, Let us make man in our image,
after our likeness and let them have dominion
Genesis 1:26a

When Adam was created, he functioned just like His Father God. He had the intellect, attitude, characteristics and nature to rule and dominate the earth as His Father ruled the heavens because his Father passed on Who He is to Adam.

The Spirit of God hath made me, and the
breath of the Almighty hath given me life
Job 33:4

Once God created Adam he, Adam, was to come into agreement with the plan of God to procreate and pass on all he had to the next generation in order for the generations to come to function in the same manner as their Father-God.

And God blessed them, and God said unto
them, Be fruitful, and multiply, and replenish
the earth, and subdue it: and have dominion
over the fish of the sea, and over the fowl of
the air, and over every living thing that moveth
upon the earth
Genesis 1:28

When we examine the scriptures after the fall we see an ongoing theme revealing the intense desire of God to reestablish His original plan of having a family in the earth. Like a father who has lost his child, He searches diligently to recover His lost offspring. And when He has found him or her, He commands heaven to rejoice with Him when His child returns, not to the church or organization, but to Him.

*I say unto you, there is joy in the presence of
the angels of God over one sinner that
repenteth
Luke 15:10*

In Hebrew, family is translated as, *a circle of
relatives.* It speaks of an unbroken line of people, tribe, or
nation whose generational connection always traces back to
the beginning, or in this case, the father, which is the
beginning of the circle's existence. The circle could be small
or it could be very large. But no matter how big or small the
circle may be it will always bring us back to the one that
created it. This circle is an eternal bond that, if you follow it,
will always return to reveal its creator.

The ways of my daughter reveal me as her father

When I watch my daughter, I am taken aback by how
much she acts like me. I see so many of my ways in her,
some good and some not so good. Some I thank God for
and some ways that compelled me to call my mother and
apologize to her for the many times I drove her crazy.

I mentioned earlier an incident in church when my
daughter was sitting on my lap and one of the assistant
pastors was tickled to death at how we both were sitting and
looking in the exact same manner. I watch how she eats, her
artistic abilities, how she rationalizes things, her cravings,
her temperament, even her goals can cause one who knows
me to look at her and immediately see me as her father.

As it is in the natural, so it is in the spiritual. When
we're born into the kingdom of God we take on the ways of
the Creator and the more we walk out those ways, the more
the Lord is reinforced within us.

The Power of Agreement

The circle broken by sin

And the LORD God commanded the man,
saying, Of every tree of the garden thou
mayest freely eat: But of the tree of the
knowledge of good and evil, thou shalt not eat
of it: for in the day that thou eatest thereof thou
shalt surely die
Genesis 2:16,17

When Adam sinned, the circle was broken. It became fragmented and dislocated. Instead of Adam birthing a generation who were to be the visible image of God in the earth, he would birth a sinful, sin-filled, idolatrous, and rebellious people eternally dislocated from the circle of God's love, plan and purpose. These people (you and I) who were supposed to walk in the character and nature of God from the very beginning, now walk in the circle of the image and likeness of their sinful father Adam. When Adam sinned, we became a people birthed into a circle filled with pride, idolatry, selfishness, and a thirst for self gratification.

I shared in my first book, *"Resting in The Fire of God"* That the first abortion didn't begin in 1973 when the Supreme Court passed the law, Roe v. Wade, legalizing abortion; it began when Adam rebelled against the commandments of his Father-God; and through his disobedience performed the greatest mass murder in the history of all mankind which is still taking place even to this very day. What do I mean? Every time a child is born into this world they are born into a spiritually dead condition.

For as in Adam all die
I Corinthians 15:22a

The law-A temporary solution

*Nevertheless death reigned from Adam to
Moses, even over them that had not sinned
after the similitude of Adam's transgression,
who is the figure of him that was to come
Romans 5:14*

When the law was instituted by God through Moses, it was a temporary solution to an eternal problem. All who were able to keep the law were consider righteous in the eyes of God. Those who were not able or didn't want to keep the law were judge by God through the law.

*For not the hearers of the law are just before
God, but the doers of the law shall be justified
Romans 2:13*

The law was a bridge for all who came into agreement with it would cross over into the circle of God where they could enjoy the love, peace, joy, and fellowship of a loving Father. It was a standard in which everyone could measure their lives and walk with God. All who maintained their walk according to the law lived under the umbrella of God's favor, love, provision, blessings, and protection.

*But his delight is in the law of the LORD; and in
his law doth he meditate day and night. And he
shall be like a tree planted by the rivers of
water, that bringeth forth his fruit in his season;
his leaf also shall not wither; and whatsoever
he doeth shall prosper
Psalm 1:2,3*

The Power of Agreement

But as much as the law brought Israel to a place where they could experience the presence and blessings of God, it was not the ultimate solution to the sin that initially broke the circle of God.

Lord Jesus comes and reveals the ways of Father God

In the fullness of time, Christ Jesus comes in the likeness of sinful man but also in the image of the Father. He was the son of man and the Son of God at the same time. This is an awesome revelation.

During His earthly ministry He came to do 2 of a multitude of things for the Father. The first thing He did was, He came so we can see our heavenly Father in all of His glory and splendor. Lord Jesus was the only person that walked this earth that revealed flawlessly the full character and nature of God-the Father. In all of His ways, acts, words, and decisions, He revealed the Father.

...he that hath seen me hath seen the Father...
John 14:9

Through this aspect of His 31/2 year earthly ministry, He showed us the Father, but he also showed us the second thing. He showed us who we are supposed to be. He was the living example of what mankind was supposed to look, act, and be. He showed us the manner in which we were to walk and talk. He showed us the dominion we have over all of creation, the authority we possess over the kingdom of darkness, and the love and compassion we were to have towards humanity and the uncompromising standard of being a child of the King. He came so that we can become who we are-the image and likeness of God in the earth.

64

Jesus Christ repairs the circle

*For what the law could not do, in that it was
weak through the flesh, God sending his own
Son in the likeness of sinful flesh, and for sin,
condemned sin in the flesh: That the
righteousness of the law might be fulfilled in us,
who walk not after the flesh, but after the Spirit.
Romans 8:3,4*

I am thoroughly convinced there is absolutely no conceivable way that in our lifetime, through the abundance of our abilities, nor the accumulation of our provision, can we ever sufficiently give Lord Jesus the gratitude, honor, appreciation, praise, and worship due to Him. What He has done for us through His sacrifice on the cross for the sin of all mankind, past, present & future is beyond estimation. He is truly worthy of our praise, worship, and obedience without question or reservation.

The law was a temporary solution for the children of Israel to the eternal problem of being separated from God. It was a pacifier, not just for man, but for God. He needed to set the law in place until the eternal solution came to reestablish the circle as it was in the beginning. That eternal solution is obviously Christ. He is the true repairer of the breach.

*Moreover the light of the moon shall be as the
light of the sun, and the light of the sun shall be
sevenfold, as the light of seven days, in the
day that the LORD bindeth up the breach of his
people, and healeth the stroke of their wound.
Isaiah 30:26*

The Power of Agreement

As the law was a temporary solution to the eternal problem of sin, Christ came to earth as the eternal solution to sin and the restorer of the family circle. Through His death, burial, & resurrection, He became the door for Israel to come back into alignment with the original plan of God's desire to produce a family of people walking in His image and likeness, demonstrating His power, love, and authority in the earth.

The restored generation of God through Christ

A seed shall serve him; it shall be accounted to the Lord for a generation. They shall come, and shall declare his righteousness unto a people that shall be born, that he hath done this
Psalm 22:30,31

As we are invited into agreement with the restored plan of God through Christ, something awesome happens. As we come into agreement with God through Christ, and are restored to the family circle, the character and nature of God through the baptism of the Holy Spirit is released into our hearts and minds, causing us to think, act, and live as the children created in the image and likeness of God. As we practice our new walk with God, the very presence and power of God is released and in the lives of His family which is the evidence or witnessed to all who encounter us that we have been restored back to the family circle of Almighty God.

It is the presence and power of God, operating in the lives of His children, revealing the blessing, favor, and love of Father God that reveals our place in the family. It isn't enough to say you're in the family, it must be seen.

Generational Agreement

*Therefore say, Thus saith the Lord GOD; I will
even gather you from the people, and
assemble you out of the countries where ye
have been scattered, and I will give you the
land of Israel. And they shall come thither, and
they shall take away all the detestable things
thereof and all the abominations thereof from
thence. And I will give them one heart, and I
will put a new spirit within you; and I will take
the stony heart out of their flesh, and will give
them a heart of flesh: That they may walk in my
statutes, and keep mine ordinances, and do
them: and they shall be my people, and I will
be their God
Ezekiel 11:17-20*

*But ye shall receive power, after that the Holy
Ghost is come upon you: and ye shall be
witnesses unto me both in Jerusalem, and in
all Judea, and in Samaria, and unto the
uttermost part of the earth
Acts 1:8*

*For ye are the temple of the living God; as God
hath said, I will dwell in them, and walk in
them; and I will be their God, and they shall be
my people
II Corinthians 6:16*

As we come into agreement with the divine will of God
and enter into His family, our natural ways we've been
reared up in are done away with. That doesn't mean we're
no longer associated with of our natural family.

The Power of Agreement

But we no longer live by the ways and will of our earthly generation but by our new divine generation reestablished by God through Lord Jesus (I Peter 2:9,10). When we come into agreement with and walk in God's restored generation through Christ, our new nature overrides our old nature thus releasing the divine presence of God into our lives and bringing us into a new dimension and perspective of life and godliness (II Peter 1:3,4). We no longer act like the old adamic family. But all of those ways are now done away with in and through Christ (II Corinthians 5:17).

Coming into agreement with God's restored generation gives us the ability to demonstrate the power of God in the earth through the operation of the Holy Spirit. As we unit with the flow and operation of God-the Holy Spirit He gives us unlimited abilities according to His purpose and plans pertaining to the kingdom.

And I, brethren, when I came to you, came not with excellency of speech or of wisdom, declaring unto you the testimony of God. For I determined not to know any thing among you, save Jesus Christ, and him crucified. And I was with you in weakness, and in fear, and in much trembling. And my speech and my preaching was not with enticing words of man's wisdom, but in demonstration of the Spirit and of power: That your faith should not stand I thewisdom of men, but in the power of God
I Corinthians 2:1-5

I can do all things through Christ which strengtheneth me
Philippians 4:13

Generational Agreements

In April of 1904, the Holy Spirit exploded on the scene in California on Bonnie Bray Street, upon a small group of people, in a little home, lead by a one-eyed pastor named William Seymour. One of the members named Jenny Moore, who would later become pastor Seymour's wife, when she was filled with the Holy Spirit, began to play the piano, having never had lessons of any kind and sang beautifully in the Hebrew language, not knowing any foreign languages.

Not long after the move of God began and the people of God moved from Bonnie Bray Street to Azusa Street, a young reporter, not of this country, working for a local newspaper, was given the assignment of going to the services to report and write in a disparaging nature on the events taking place on Azusa Street. As he sat in the back of the sanctuary, he watched many of God's people manifesting the power of God in various ways. Then, while pastor Seymour was sharing God's word, a young lady in the congregation, overshadowed by the Holy Spirit, began to speak in an unknown tongue for several minutes. When the service was completed, the young reporter managed to find the young lady who spoke in tongues and asked her where she learned to speak in that language. The young lady told him she had never learned to speak in any type of language. It was later said that the language the young lady spoke in by the Holy Spirit was the young reporter's native language. And she spoke by the Holy Spirit all he ever did in his life.

After this experience, the young reporter gave his life to the Lord and decided not to do the report on the services.

As I mentioned earlier, when we come into agreement with the reestablished family of God, we step out of one way of thinking and doing and we come into another.

Where there was once fear, hatred, and torment, there is now power, love, and a sound mind (II Timothy 1:7).

The Power of Agreement

Where there was once depression, there is now joy (Psalm 16:11). Where there was sickness and destruction, there is now prosperity and divine health (Psalm 107:20). And where there was once death and sadness there is now victory (Isaiah 25:8).

The invitation to join the circle

And the Spirit and the bride say, Come. And let him that heareth say, Come. And let him that is athirst come. And whosoever will, let him take the water of life freely
Revelation 22:17

I believe this invitation isn't relegated to those who are unsaved. I believe throughout the body of Christ there are millions of men, women, boys, and girls who have yet to truly give themselves over to the complete control of the Holy Spirit. And because of the diverse denominational and doctrinal differences, religious, tradition and dysfunctions looming throughout Lord Jesus' church, He is still calling out to His people to come into agreement with what He's made ready for us, not just by faith, but in reality. Until we give ourselves over to the complete will of God we'll never fulfill all that Christ has prophesied concerning His church.

We are the generation of God. We are the ones whom God is calling into His fullness and as we do this we will truly reveal the image and likeness of God in the earth.

Let us hear what the Spirit is saying unto His people and give heed to it. Not just for our benefit, but all for His glory.

70

Chapter 7
Agreement with Seasons

And of the children of Issachar, which were
men that had understanding of the times, to
know what Israel ought to do
I Chronicles 12:32a

Understanding seasons is one of the most important aspects of our walk with God. Unless we understand seasons, we're lost, blind, and vulnerable to satan. Each season has a word from God within it which requires us to understand and submit to, to establish Christ in the earth.

It is important to know that each season has its own specific purpose which causes our destiny to manifest and evolve to a greater, more powerful reality. But one of the important elements to understand about seasons is that for every season we come into, go through, and fulfill, it is also designed to prepare us for the next season. And each season reveals Christ in greater depth and clarity. Each season releases the glory of God in a more power way. For how can we go from one realm of glory to another realm of glory except we understand seasons?

And of the children of Issachar, which were
men that had understanding of the times, to
know what Israel ought to do
I Chronicles 12:32

The word season in the Greek means, *An appointed time.* There is an appointed time in God that He desires to have specific aspects of His plan fulfilled in the lives of His people and His universal plan for mankind. Each appointed time in a season requires our participation as co-laborers with God to see the desires of His heart fulfilled.

The Power of Agreement

Seasons are an ordained time established before the foundations of the world by God where He moves by His Spirit to fulfill both individual and corporate prophetic words within that preordained season.

God has certain things He desires to fulfill in the earth at certain moments in time. Like a chess piece, He positions His people by His Spirit and places them in preordained positions within preordained moments in time we call seasons. God, in His omniscience, requires us to come into agreement with Him to see His plan within each season accomplished and manifested in the earth in the time in which He has appointed, not only for our own personal benefit, not only for the benefit of the church at large, but for His ultimately universal will to be done in the earth.

To miss a season in God is one of the most tragic, if not the most tragic moments in God's plan for His kingdom. Because seasons are missed, it causes a ripple effect to take place throughout humanity and forces God to make major unnecessary adjust. There are souls that God wants to save through us. There are people that need to be healed and delivered through us. And there are blessings God wants to release. Whether we believe it or not what happens to each of us affects others. But whether it's with or without our cooperation, God's plan will be fulfilled in the earth.

Remember the former things of old: for I am God, and there is none else; I am God, and there is none like me, Declaring the end from the beginning, and from ancient times the things that are not yet done, saying, My counsel shall stand, and I will do all my pleasure
Isaiah 46:9,10

Being sensitive to the changing times

*And it came to pass after many days, that the
word of the LORD came to Elijah in the third
year, saying, Go, show thyself unto Ahab; and I
will send rain upon the earth…And Elijah said
unto Ahab, Get thee up, eat and drink; for there
is a sound of abundance of rain… And Elijah
went up to the top of Carmel; and he cast
himself down upon the earth, and put his face
between his knees, And said to his servant, Go
up now, look toward the sea. And he went up,
and looked, and said, There is nothing. And he
said, Go again seven times. And it came to
pass at the seventh time, that he said, Behold,
there ariseth a little cloud out of the sea, like a
man's hand. And he said, Go up, say unto
Ahab, Prepare thy chariot, and get thee down,
that the rain stop thee not. And it came to pass
in the meanwhile, that the heaven was black
with clouds and wind, and there was a great
rain
I Kings 18:1,41-45*

As God's people, you and I must be sensitive to and
come into agreement as co-laborers with God-the Holy Spirit
to see the kingdom of God established and completely fill
and dominate the earth. Where there is not sensitivity
between us and the move of God, there is no cohesiveness.

From a prophetic perspective it is vital to understand
the changing times and all that pertains to the shifting from
one season to the next. Most importantly, we must see the
hand of the Lord within each changing paradigm.

The Power of Agreement

I pray and trust that as you read on and study in your own personal time, God-the Holy Spirit will bring you and I into an even deeper sensitivity to move as He moves and to understand the importance of walking with Him in and through various seasons set before us. Lets look at how God and His prophet, Elijah, worked together to move from one season to the next by examining I Kings 18:1,41-45.

And it came to pass after many days

The scriptures begins by saying, *And it came to pass after many days*. Three and half years ago, God sent the prophet Elijah to boldly stand before king Ahab and proclaimed there would be no rain in the land except at his word (I Kings 17:1). After this season, the Lord comes to Elijah and informs him this season of famine and drought has come to an end. I'm going to send an abundance of rain into the land. Go and stand before Ahab again and proclaim my word.

Seasons vary not only in purpose but in time. There are some seasons in which God does a quick work. And there are some seasons which seem to be an eternity. But the important element in each season isn't so much the time of each season, but the fulfillment of the will of God within each season. It is not for us to determine the length of a season. This privilege lies within the sovereign will of God. Our responsibility is to follow the plan God has laid out within that season and see to it that it is accomplished.

And he said unto them, It is not for you to know
the times or the seasons, which the Father
hath put in his own power
Acts 1:7

We must understand no season is to our benefit, nor to the glory of God unless every jot and tittle is fulfilled in it. Each ordained sequence of events leads to another sequence of events which brings about a release of the glory of God in the earth. Notice God, after 31/2 years, tells Elijah to go before Ahab. Elijah's obedience to the instructions of God was absolutely essential to set up the next event which was to challenge the prophets of baal in the demonstration of power. The fulfillment of this event turned the entire nation of Israel back to God. This event lead to the effectual prayer of Elijah (James 5:16), which caused the heavens to go black and release an abundance of rain in the land, which brought the season of famine and drought to an end. Unless Elijah obeyed God within this season, the prophets of baal would not have been destroyed, the children of Israel would have not rededicated themselves back to God, and the land would not have received the much needed rain.

And of the children of Issachar, which were
men that had understanding of the times, to
know what Israel ought to do
I Chronicles 12:32

God takes no pleasure in a season in which what He's ordained to be accomplished isn't fulfilled. The unwillingness to do all that God has ordained puts God behind schedule and makes us unprepared for the tasks we've been charge to accomplish. For us to resist the will of God is to not only resist our purpose, but we resist God.

Yea, they turned back and tempted God, and
limited the Holy One of Israel
Psalm 78:41

The Power of Agreement

As we read I Kings 18 we can notice within the spirit of the scriptures there are silent instructions given to the prophet to bring about God's desired result. This is being sensitive to the Spirit of God. There was nothing verbally mentioned about challenging the prophets of baal. There was nothing mentioned about where the challenge was to take place. There was nothing mentioned about how to set up the sacrifice. There wasn't even anything mentioned that the sending of the rain required Elijah to petition God for it. This is what I mean by being sensitive to the Spirit of God and His plans within each season and co-laboring with Him to see the desires of His heart fulfilled within it.

Go, show thyself unto Ahab; and I will send rain upon the earth

I am absolutely convinced a child of God should never be caught off guard when it comes to God's will being done. When God does something in the earth it should never take us aback. Whether it's saving a soul, healing the afflicted, deliver the oppressed, changing the weather, or opening doors, nothing should take us by surprise in God. If this happens it is for 2 reasons. One, the person is a new believer and hasn't yet come into an intimate relationship with the Holy Spirit. And the second is because the believer doesn't have an intimate relationship with the Holy Spirit. The first is understandable. The second is unacceptable. For the Lord does nothing without letting us know in advance.

Howbeit when he, the Spirit of truth, is come, he will guide you into all truth...and he will show you things to come
John 16:13

Whether it involves the entire body of Christ or it's on a personal level, the Lord will without fail inform us of His intentions. This is vital to the fulfillment of the season we're in and for the ushering in of the next season. This is because He desires our participation in the fulfillment of His plan. This is an awesome privilege. He said to Elijah, *Go, show thyself unto Ahab; and I will send rain upon the earth.* The desire of the Lord to send rain could not be realized without the prophet's willingness to position himself before the rebellious king. Our position, both geographically and spiritually, is so important to the fulfillment of seasons it cannot be overstated. Positioning in the work of God must be taken very seriously if the plans and purposes of God are going to manifest in the earth. We cannot minimize this facet of God's plan because it doesn't line up with our selfish desires. It really baffles me to see men and women who profess to love God and yet are unwilling to do His will. Many of us put our own fleshly desires before the desires of God. And if His plans doesn't line up with ours we disregard His or at the least we put it off thinking God will wait until we get around to doing His will. This type of thinking is evidence of our lack of reverence and devotion to the Lord and His plan for mankind. This is about God, not about us.

Our position and obedience to the plan of God within each season is key to releasing the power of God in the earth. Many of God's people miss some awesome encounters with God by not being sensitive to the move of the Holy Spirit. Elijah's obedience to position himself before Ahab was key to the release the rain. The bible says in Song of Solomon 2:15, *the little foxes, that spoil the vines.* It is the things we see as insignificant that God sees as vital to the His will being done. Being at Sunday service or at a street corner, sensitivity to God is vital to fulfillment of His will.

The Power of Agreement

And Elijah went up to the top of Carmel;
and he cast himself down upon the earth,
and put his face between his knees

Of all the essential keys to ensure the successful fulfillment of a season, the most important key is prayer. Rather than share my own person feelings on prayer, I want to share some historic remarks from those giants of prayer whose fervent petitions shaped the world and the kingdom of God in their day, in our time, and the world to come.

The very life and prosperity of God's cause-
even its very existence-depends on prayer.
And the advance and triumph of His cause
depend on one thing: that we ask Him
E.M. Bounds

My creed leads me to think that prayer is
efficacious, and surely a day's asking God to
overrule all events for good is not lost
James Gilmour

We must remember that the goal of prayer is
the ear of God. Unless that is gained, the
prayer has utterly failed. The uttering of it may
have kindled devotional feeling in our minds,
the hearing of it may have comforted and
strengthened the hearts of those with whom we
have prayed, but if the prayer has not gained
the heart of God, it has failed in its essential
purpose
Charles Spurgeon

The prayers of holy men appease God's wrath, drive away temptations, resist and overcome the devil, procure the ministry and service of angels, rescind the decrees of God. Prayer cures sickness and obtains pardon; it arrests the sun in its course and stays the wheels of the chariot of the moon; it rules over all gods and opens and shuts the storehouses of rain; it unlocks the cabinet of the womb and quenches the violence of fire; it stops the mouths of lions and reconciles our sufferings and weak faculties with the violence of torments and violence of persecution; it pleases God and supplies all our need
Jeremy Taylor

In God's name, I beech you, let prayer nourish your soul as your meals nourish your body. Let your fixed seasons of prayer keep you in God's presence through the day, and may His presence frequently remembered through it be an ever fresh spring of prayer. Such a brief, loving recollection of God renews a man's whole being, quiets his passions, supplies light and counsel in difficulty, gradually subdues the temper, and...gives it up to the possession of God
Fe'nelon

I would rather train twenty men to pray, than a thousand to preach; - A minister's highest mission ought to be to teach his people to pray
H. MacGregor

The Power of Agreement

*And Elijah went up to the top of Carmel; and he
cast himself down upon the earth, and put his
face between his knees
I Kings 18:42*

What makes prayer so powerful isn't the mere act of prayer, but the will of God being prayed. Unless we understand what the will of the Lord is we are uttering empty petitions.

*Wherefore be ye not unwise, but
understanding what the will of the Lord is
Ephesians 5:17*

To know what the will of God is requires us to be intimate with God. Prayer is an intimate, passionate conversation with the Almighty. The closer we are to the Lord the more He opens His heart to reveal His desires to us until we become so consumed with Him that His desires become our desires and we cry out to God from His heart.

In every season we experience, God will not always reveal every aspect of the moment. But as we go forward to fulfill His will He reveals a portion of the overall plan to us and the process to see it fulfilled. And the maturity of God's plan is contingent upon our petition to Him. No aspect of God's overall plan can be fulfilled apart from prayer. We can be a hearer and a doer of the word but unless prayer is the epicenter of our endeavors we lack the staying power to see it through. The bible says Elijah fell to the grown in prayer and instructed his servant to go and look toward the sea. If Elijah didn't know the will of God, was not close to God and diligent in prayer, when the servant came and told him there was nothing he would probably have given up.

And this is where many of us come short of our prize. Because we don't see the results in the time we think appropriate we become discouraged and disappointed and often times give up in our pursuits in petitioning God. I myself have been guilty of this dysfunction on many occasions. But what I love about Elijah is it was his importunacy in prayer that brought forth the will of God. Even when the prophet of God received 6 negative reports he prayed until the rain came.

The effectual fervent prayer of a righteous man
availeth much
James 5:16b

We must also understand that prayer produces 2 things within every season. Prayer not only brings answers but it also sets the stage for the manifestation of the answer. Prayer positions and repositions. It heals and reconnects that which as been damaged and dislocated. It blows away the dust off of ancient promises and revives our passion to see them fulfilled. The position and repositioning through prayer is essential in order to bring about the necessary order for the fulfillment of the heart of God.

And they shall build the old wastes, they shall
raise up the former desolations, and they shall
repair the waste cities, the desolations of many
generations
Isaiah 61:4

The other thing that prayer produces is warfare. When we pray according to the will of God we disrupt the realm of the spirit and the plans and schemes of the enemy.

The Power of Agreement

You and I as believers must understand the power that exists within us. When we cry out to God we literally shake the heavens. Like an earthquake brings down mountains causing great damage or causes millions of tons of ocean water to go beyond its banks and destroy regions, our prayers literally sends shockwaves through the realm of heaven. And when this takes place it disrupts the order of satan. Daniel understood this and experienced it first hand what happens when you pray according to the will of God the level of warfare you will encounter.

> *Then said he unto me, Fear not, Daniel: for from the first day that thou didst set thine heart to understand, and to chasten thyself before thy God, thy words were heard, and I am come for thy words. But the prince of the kingdom of Persia withstood me one and twenty days: but, lo, Michael, one of the chief princes, came to help me; and I remained there with the kings of Persia. Now I am come to make thee understand what shall befall thy people in the latter days: for yet the vision is for many days.*
> Daniel 10:12-14

There is nothing more frightful and dangerous to the enemy than a praying man or woman of God. A person passionate and persistent in prayer is the most destructive instrument in the hand of God and the means to the downfall of the kingdom of darkness. This is why prophets, intercessors, and prayer warriors are attacked frequently. If the enemy can distract us with financial woes, health problems, family dysfunctions, etc, he can disrupt us in prayer in order to keep his kingdom in operation.

Agreement with Seasons

Understanding what the will of God is in each season is important but being prepared for warfare from satan is important as well. Like any war or just endeavoring to achieve a goal, we will have and must expect opposition. But just as prayer is the key to fulfilling the will of God, it's also the key to defeating the enemy.

I can recall not long ago during our Sunday service encountering the enemy. We were in the midst of praise and worship. Many of us were focused on praising and worshipping God. But God has taught me over the years how to watch, pray, praise, and worship at the same time.

During this time a man we know walked into the sanctuary and immediately I saw several spirits upon him sent to disrupt what was taking place in the service. I was instantly instructed of the Lord to begin praying in the Spirit. This warfare went on for a while when suddenly there was a release. I saw the spirits leave and I was able to focus on praise and worship again. After the service I went to my pastor and shared with her what I saw. She shared with me that she saw the same thing and began to pray as well. Not only did we disrupt the plans of the enemy, God saved this man's life through our prayer as well. As we discussed the matter further my pastor and I saw the spirit of death working with a suicidal spirit to destroy this man. We didn't lay hands, we didn't scream at the man or the demons. We went into the sprit through prayer and God gave us the victory.

I thank God for my pastor. She has been my mentor and friend for many years, even before she became a pastor she and I were good friends. We've been in many spiritual battles over the years. We've done everything from casting out demons tormenting a child to cleansing houses, to changing the weather. And in all of these experiences we've come to realize that without prayer we wouldn't be here.

83

The Power of Agreement

I encourage you in the name of the Lord Jesus Christ, to endeavor to know what the will of the Lord is in your life. Make prayer, along with the word of God your foundation and your passion. Know what season you're in and all that God desires to do in it.

Seasons are beautiful and refreshing. They bring forth new and exciting experiences and bring us into greater maturity and intimacy with our Lord.

Embrace your seasons. Cry out to God and allow Him to show the great and mighty things He has in store for you in the season you're about to experience. I promise you, you won't regret it.

Chapter 8
Agreement with God-The Holy Spirit

*And I, brethren, when I came to you, came not
with excellency of speech or of wisdom,
declaring unto you the testimony of God. For I
determined not to know any thing among you,
save Jesus Christ, and him crucified. And I was
with you in weakness, and in fear, and in much
trembling. And my speech and my preaching
was not with enticing words of man's wisdom,
but in demonstration of the Spirit and of power:
That your faith should not stand in the wisdom
of men, but in the power of God
I Corinthians 2:1-5*

The world is saturated with religion. Hundreds of
various forms of faiths are in every aspect of society. Some
visible, some not. Some liberal and some conservative.
Some radical and some fundamental. People around the
world are inundated with all forms of religious information
which produce more confusion rather than clarity. People are
hungry for truth but are apprehensive to embrace any
particular faith for fear of being deceived and lead down a
path they may never be able to recover from.

History is saturated with stories of people who
became leaders of some faith or religious organization that
brought about death and destruction and have contributed to
the fear people have towards searching and finding out what
is the truth. And it is sad to say that even the church has
contributed to the chaos.

But with all of the various religions, cults, and occults
in operation in the world the one element that separates
Christianity from all others is the presence, power, and
operation of God-the Holy Spirit.

85

The Power of Agreement

The late George Smeaton of Scotland expressed the importance of the divine presence and work of the Holy Spirit by saying:

"Wherever Christianity has been a living power, the doctrine of the Holy Spirit has uniformly been regarded, equally with the Atonement and Justification by faith, as the article of a standing or falling church. The distinctive feature of Christianity as it addresses itself to man's experience, is the work of the Spirit, which not only elevates it far above all philosophical speculation, but also above every other form of religion."

The one Person that sets Christianity far above all other so-called faiths is the presence and operation of the Holy Spirit. Without Him Christianity would just be another faith in a genre of other faiths claiming to be the true faith.

For wherein shall it be known here that I and thy people have found grace in thy sight? is it not in that thou goest with us? so shall we be separated, I and thy people, from all the people that are upon the face of the earth
Exodus 33:16

If Christians are going to truly represent our Lord and Savior, Jesus Christ, we are going to have to come into agreement with God-the Holy Spirit and all that He's been sent here to do with, in, and through us.

Agreement with God-The Holy Spirit

To think we can entice men with our eloquent words, fancy preaching, singing, shouting, and religious professions is true evidence of our ignorance, arrogance, and lack of understanding of what it means to walk in the Spirit.

The apostle Paul, in I Corinthians chapter 2, verses 4 and 5, gives us a clear understanding of what the deciding factor is to reach a society that still walk in spiritual indecisiveness, which is the demonstration of the Spirit.

The word demonstration in the Greek means, *manifestation, to show forth or to exhibit.* It is the willingness to allow the Spirit of God to manifest Himself through our earthen vessels to show forth and exhibit His character, nature, power, love, and will to mankind. But in order for this to be done we must submit our will and come into agreement with His will.

Teach me to do thy will; for thou art my God:
thy spirit is good; lead me into the land of
uprightness
Psalm 143:10

The Holy Spirit is the enabling force that gives us the ability to perform all the will of God. There is nothing we can't do when we're moving in a yielded mindset with the Holy Spirit. The only limitations that exist between us and the Holy Spirit is our limited thinking and unwillingness to relinquish control to Him. When I can completely submit to the presence and operation of the Holy Spirit there's nothing that He can't do through us and nothing we can't do through Him.

I can do all things through Christ which
strengtheneth me
Philippians 4:13

The Power of Agreement

The purpose for Christ's sacrifice wasn't just the dying for our sins, but for the release of the Holy Spirit into the world. Christ expressed the importance of His departure from this world in order for the Holy Spirit to come to institute the will of the Father in the earth. He is the means by which the world is reproved of sin, righteousness is established, and reconciliation is made between the Father and the lost.

> *Nevertheless I tell you the truth; It is expedient for you that I go away: for if I go not away, the Comforter will not come unto you; but if I depart, I will send him unto you. And when he is come, he will reprove the world of sin, and of righteousness, and of judgment: Of sin, because they believe not on me; Of righteousness, because I go to my Father, and ye see me no more; Of judgment, because the prince of this world is judged*
> *John 16:7-11*

Samuel Chadwick shared this thought on the subject of the Holy Spirit:

> *"The gift of the Spirit is the crowning mercy of God in Christ Jesus. It was for this all the rest was. The Incarnation and Crucifixion, the Resurrection and Ascension were all preparatory to Pentecost. Without the gift of the Holy Spirit all the rest would be useless. The great thing in Christianity is the gift of the Spirit. The essential, vital, central element in the life of the soul and the work of the Church is the Person of the Spirit"*

88

Agreement with God-The Holy Spirit

It is only by the influence of God-the Holy Spirit that any heavenly revelation and communication can be conveyed. It is by the Holy Spirit that the heart of God is shared and the secrets of men's hearts are revealed, thus causing their faith to be founded solely upon the demonstration and power of God and not the wisdom and intellect of man.

> *And my speech and my preaching was not with enticing words of man's wisdom, but in demonstration of the Spirit and of power: That your faith should not stand in the wisdom of men, but in the power of God*
> *I Corinthians 2:4,5*

The importance of coming into agreement with the Holy Spirit can never be overstated nor exhausted. If we as believers are ever going to come into the knowledge of the truth and be conformed to the image of Christ, this will only be accomplished by yielding to the inner working of God-the Holy Spirit. But we must come into agreement with Him and submit to His will being done in our lives.

The greatest need of the Church in this hour is to **"submit to God-the Holy Spirit and hear what He is saying unto the Church."** Only through the communication of the Spirit can we know the heart of the Father. But for us to hear the heart of the Father we must have an ear to hear what the Holy Spirit is saying. And only in union with the Spirit can we develop a holy ear to commune with Him.

I mentioned earlier that there is no limit to the operation of the Holy Spirit in the life of a believer completely given over to His will. The only limitation in relation to the Spirit is our limited thinking and resistance to Him.

The Power of Agreement

The apostle Paul wrote to the Ephesians that he was praying for them that they would have an experience with God that would be beyond comprehension. And I believe this same prayer is the will of the Lord for us as well. He said this in chapter 3 of Ephesians in the Amplified Version:

For this reason [seeing the greatness of this plan by which you are built together in Christ], I bow my knees before the Father of our Lord Jesus Christ, for Whom every family in heaven and on earth is named [that Father from Whom all fatherhood takes its title and derives its name]. May He grant you out of the rich treasury of His glory to be strengthened and reinforced with mighty power in the inner man by the [Holy] Spirit [Himself indwelling your innermost being and personality]. May Christ through your faith [actually] dwell (settle down, abide, make His permanent home) in your hearts! May you be rooted deep in love and founded securely on love, That you may have the power and be strong to apprehend and grasp with all the saints [God's devoted people, the experience of that love] what is the breadth and length and height and depth [of it]; [That you may really come to know [practically, through experience for yourselves] the love of Christ, which far surpasses mere knowledge [without experience]; that you may be filled [through all your being] unto all the fullness of God[may have the richest measure of the divine Presence, and become a body wholly filled and flooded with God Himself]!

Can you imagine reaching such a level of oneness with the Lord that every fiber of your entire being is completely consumed with the glory and power of Almighty God Himself? Can you believe this is God's will for His people? Or are you stuck in a religious mindset of climbing up the rough side of the mountain and just holding on until Christ returns? Is that enough for you? I truly hope not.

There is a large portion of the body of Christ that hasn't caught this revelation of God's desire to bring His people into a realm of oneness with Him by His Spirit. We are called to this realm of limitless wonder, beauty, power, and glory. This is the very reason for Lord Jesus' sacrifice. This was the very plan of God from the foundation of the world, to conform us into the image of God, not in the by and by, but in the here and now.

I remember many years ago, I was attending a bible school. During a class discussion on the book of Hebrews, I began to read verses 1 through 3 of chapter 6:

Therefore leaving the principles of the doctrine of Christ, let us go on unto perfection; not laying again the foundation of repentance from dead works, and of faith toward God, Of the doctrine of baptisms, and of laying on of hands, and of resurrection of the dead, and of eternal judgment. And this will we do, if God permit
Hebrews 6:1-6

As I read this passage of scripture, I was captured by the words *"let us go on unto perfection."* As I meditated on this portion of scripture, the Holy Spirit began to impart to me a revelation that has never left me. That revelation was His desire to bring His people into a place of oneness with Him.

The Power of Agreement

The Lord showed me He was calling His people to a place of perfection which can only be realized through walking in oneness with His Spirit. Where His ways and thoughts would become our ways and thoughts. That being seated with Him in heavenly places was the will of the Father for His people to experience now. As we come into agreement with the word in Philippians 2:5, which says:

Let this mind be in you, which was also in
Christ Jesus

We would come into a realm of glory and a paradigm of thought equal with Christ when He walked the earth. That we would walk in a perfected state, flawless in thought, character, and deeds.

[That you may really come to know [practically,
through experience for yourselves] the love of
Christ, which far surpasses mere knowledge
[without experience]; that you may be filled
[through all your being] unto all the fullness of
God[may have the richest measure of the
divine Presence, and become a body wholly
filled and flooded with God Himself]!
Ephesians 3:19
The Amplified Version

But I say, walk and live [habitually] in the [Holy]
Spirit [responsive to and controlled and guided
by the Spirit]; then you will certainly not gratify
the cravings and desires of the flesh (of human
nature without God)…

Agreement with God-The Holy Spirit

If we live by the [Holy] Spirit, let us also walk by
the Spirit, [if by the Holy Spirit we have our life
in God, let us go forward walking in line, our
conduct controlled by the Spirit.]
Galatians 5:16,25
The Amplified Version

Well in my excitement I shared this with the class (not asking the Lord if I was supposed to). And I was torn apart by everyone in the class including the instructor. I was looked at strangely from that day on. What I had to say from that day wasn't received by all like before. Teachers began to watch me and what I was saying to make sure it was in line with what they believed. As time went on I became discouraged and even began to question myself and eventually I just let go of what God revealed.

Months later my friend (now my pastor) shared with me some teachings by a man of God named Bill Britton. He received a revelation from the Lord on the subject of the Sons of God back in the 50's. He began to teach through tapes and books on this revelation from the word of God that God was calling His people to walk in oneness with Him through His Spirit, revealing the full nature of Christ in the earth through those who would come into agreement with His will. He was calling His people to walk in the demonstration of the Spirit in unlimited dimensions. God was calling His people to divorce themselves from the false doctrine of man and satan and come into the reality of what it means to be a child of God, filled with and yielded to the Spirit of God.

When I read his teachings it was as if that revelation was resurrected within my spirit and I began studying the word with the understanding that this was God's will for me.

The Power of Agreement

God is calling us to come into agreement with His Spirit in unlimited dimensions. Remember, the only limitation is our limited thinking and understanding of our position in God through the Holy Spirit. Let's look at some attributes we as the people of God are called to walk in.

Possessing unlimited vision

The first attribute made available to us is the ability to see without limitations. There's no distance in the realm of the spirit. God gives us this gift to see that which has and is to come.

In II Kings 6:8-11, we see the king of Assyria declaring war against Israel. As the Assyrian king took counsel with his generals on how to attack Israel, God opened the eyes of the prophet, Elisha, to see all they were planning and conveyed what he saw to the king of Israel, thus destroying the plans and schemes of the enemy.

Remember I shared with you the people of God should never be caught off guard in any way shape or form because God reveals his intentions to His people (John 16:13). But as He reveals His plans to us, He also reveals the plans of the enemy that we may always be a step ahead of him in all he does. This is so vital to successful warfare. As a result of the unlimited vision Elisha operated in, Israel was able to avoid the enemy's attacks. This caused the king of Assyria to become frustrated and brought division and accusation within his circle. This is vital if we are going to be successful and victorious in all we do for our lives and ministries. The more we're united with the Holy Spirit the more vivid our vision becomes in the spirit. The more we refuse to yield to God the more blind we are to what God is doing and vulnerable to the attacks of the enemy.

This is why the body of Christ in many areas are more reactive than pro-active because we can't see what God wants to reveal to us concerning His plans as well as the intentions of the enemy.

Later in the story, the Assyrian king realized that Elisha was the cause of his plans being thwarted. He sent his army after him and when they found the prophet of God they surrounded him. When the servant of Elisha rose up that morning he was overcome with fear for what he saw in the natural. But here again we see the benefits of possessing unlimited vision.

> *And when the servant of the man of God was risen early, and gone forth, behold, a host compassed the city both with horses and chariots. And his servant said unto him, Alas, my master! how shall we do? And he answered, Fear not: for they that be with us are more than they that be with them. And Elisha prayed, and said, LORD, I pray thee, open his eyes, that he may see. And the LORD opened the eyes of the young man; and he saw: and, behold, the mountain was full of horses and chariots of fire round about Elisha*
> *II Kings 6:15-17*

This is an awesome revelation of what we have in God. If you and I can come into agreement with God-the Holy Spirit He will literally open our eyes to a dimension we've never experienced before. He has given us the ability to see in 2 dimensions (the seen and unseen) at the same time. He has given us the ability to see what was, what is, and what is to come. All we need to do is submit.

The Power of Agreement

Possessing unlimited knowledge

*For who hath known the mind of the Lord, that
he may instruct him? But we have the mind of
Christ
I Corinthians 2:16*

To come into agreement with the Lord is to yield to His way of thinking. And when we yield to His way of thinking we access knowledge beyond our natural ability to comprehend. When we come into agreement with the Holy Spirit our minds are open to His knowledge. We literally access heavenly revelation that can only be accessed through a mind united with the Spirit of the living God.

We no longer think as the world does with all of its legalistic, ritualistic, religious, limited thinking. But we come into a realm of thinking synonymous with the Lord Jesus when He walked the earth during His earthly ministry.

When we come into agreement with the Holy Spirit He reveals to us the secrets of men's hearts. This is also key to be an affective witness for Christ and leading souls into the kingdom. When you begin tell people what's in their heart, you've got their attention. They become a captive audience and are open to the gospel. People are hearing all about Lord Jesus. But now they need to see Lord Jesus in action. But again, the only way Christ can be activated is by His people coming into agreement with Him.

*But Jesus did not commit himself unto them,
because he knew all men, And needed not that
any should testify of man: for he knew what
was in man
John 2:24,25*

Agreement with God-the Holy Spirit

When we yield to the Holy Spirit His plan for mankind becomes clear to us and how it is to be implemented in the earth. We know where we're supposed to be and when to be there. We know what we're supposed to be doing in the time we're supposed to do it. We know with whom we're supposed to be connected to and implementing His plans with. No longer are we tossed to and fro as someone who has no understanding of who they are and why they're here. But we walk in a confidence that is rooted in the mind that knows what the will of the Lord is concerning us because we have and are operating in the mind of Christ.

Let this mind be in you, which was also in
Christ Jesus
Philippians 2:5

Possessing unlimited abilities

I can do all things through Christ which
strengtheneth me
Philippians 4:13

I want to share some real life accounts of men and women who came into agreement with the Holy Spirit. I pray that as you read on you will begin to see yourself operating in a dimension of unlimited abilities.

Speaking different languages

On December 31, 1900, during the night long
New Year's watch service, a student named
Agnes N. Ozman, asked her teacher, Charles
Parham, to lay hands on her and pray for her
97

to receive the baptism with the Holy Spirit accompanied by the evidence of speaking with other tongues. When he later wrote of this even, Parham said, "I laid my hands upon her and prayed. I had scarcely repeated three dozen sentences when a glory fell upon her, a halo seemed to surround her head and face, and she began speaking the Chinese language and was unable to speak English for three days. When she tried to write in English to tell us of her experience she wrote the Chinese. During these meetings, it was later claimed the students spoke in twenty one known languages, including Swedish, Russian, Bulgarian, Japanese, Norwegian, French, Hungarian, Italian, and Spanish. According to Parham, none of his students had studied any of these languages, and they were all confirmed as authentic by native speakers.

Playing instruments

In April 9, 1906, at 214 Bonnie Brae Street, the Holy Spirit fell on William Seymour and seven others and they began to speak with other tongues. One of the seven recipients of the baptism earlier in the evening was Jennie Moore…She began to play beautiful music on an old upright piano, and to sing in what people said was Hebrew. Up until that time she had never played the piano, and although she never took a lessen, she was able to play the instrument for the rest of her life.

Agreement with God-the Holy Spirit

Praying without ceasing

In 1727, in the small town of Hernhutt, 24 men and 24 women entered into covenant to pray for one hour, 24 hours a day for God's blessing on their congregation. This prayer time, which would later know as "The Hourly Intercession", went on 24 hours a day for one hundred years.

Powerful preaching

Charles G. Finney was anointed of God to "root out" and to "plant" in the Lord's vineyard, (Jer. 1:10). He was a man of intense prayer, purity and passion. "Emptied of self, he was filled with the Holy Spirit. His sermons were chain lightning, flashing conviction into the hearts of the stoutest skeptics. Simple as a child in his utterances, he sometimes startled his hearers by his unique prayers." Finney's autobiography is filled with accounts of powerful manifestations of the Spirit. On one occasion when Finney was preaching in a school house, "suddenly an awful solemnity fell upon the assembly and the congregation fell from their seats, crying for mercy." Finney said, "If I had had a sword in each hand I could not have cut them off as fast as they fell. I think the whole congregation was on their knees or prostrated in two minutes." The crying and weeping of the people was so loud that Finney's exhortation of Christ's mercy could not even be heard.

The Power of Agreement

Power manifestations

Born in 1844, Maria Woodworth-Etter lived in Lisbon, Ohio. God called her to preach at a time when people did not believe that women should preach. In fact, at this time women were not even allowed to vote. She saw the death of her little children one by one until she decided to obey Jesus Christ and go and preach the Gospel. It has been recorded that she had one of the most powerful ministries and anointings - with astounding healings, miracles and wonders - that has ever been documented in the history of the church. Reports state that she would come into a town after sleeping in a tent, and within days there would be approximately 20,000 people in her meetings. At times, God would give people working in the fields in a fifty-mile radius around her meetings visions of heaven and hell, and they would fall to the ground under tremendous conviction. It was like a "blanket" anointing that would come down upon the whole area. It has been reported that for whole blocks around her meetings, people would be falling to the ground and repenting.

When we submit to the Holy Spirit there's nothing we can't do. When we yield we can boldly say:

I can do all things through Christ which strengtheneth me
Philippians 4:13
100

Possessing unlimited finances & provision

*The silver is mine, and the gold is mine, saith
the LORD of hosts
Haggai 2:8*

Those of us called to establish the kingdom of God, who are mature enough in God, and have God's interest as a priority will come into this experience. God has called His people into abundance without measure. This is important to build the kingdom of God and be a witness of God's love and blessings. But it's not for those whose hearts are filled with greed or covetousness. God is calling His people to come into agreement with Him to release the silver and the gold into the hands of His people that will go forth and do the will of God. There's no limit to what's available to us in God.

Lord Jesus instructed Peter to go fishing and without even placing bait on the hook, a fish would attached itself to it and as he would bring it up in its mouth would be a coin to pay the taxes (Matthew 17:24-27*).*

When the woman of God came to Elisha and explained to him that the creditor was coming to take her sons because she was behind on the rent, the man of God instructed her to go and borrow as many pots as she could and take the oil that was in her house and fill the pots, pay the creditor and live off of the rest.

Elijah went to see a widow woman who was convinced she and her son was about to die because of their lack of food. The prophet of God instructed her to fix him a little cake and then feed her and her son and the barrel of meal would never run out.

And what can we say about Lord Jesus and the 2 fish and 5 loaves of bread. When we yield, there's no limit.

The Power of Agreement

Experiencing unlimited transportation

In Acts 8:37-40, we see Phillip, being led by the Holy Spirit, going to witness to a eunuch and after the eunuch received Christ as his personal Savior, Phillip was suddenly carried away by the Spirit to a another geographical location to continue his work for the Lord.

Can you imagine being in such agreement with the Lord that at any given time when we're poised to do His will, He can whisk us away to the very place to do His will and when we've done what He's instructed us we're whisked away again homeward or to another place? We'll have no need (if it's the Lord's will) for modern transportation, but we'll have the heavenly transportation of the Holy Spirit and with there being no distant in the spirit suddenly bring us to His desired location to do His will. This is very real and will become a common occurrence in the days to come.

Possessing unlimited authority

Behold, I give unto you power to tread on
serpents and scorpions, and over all the power
of the enemy: and nothing shall by any means
hurt you
Luke 10:19

You and I are royalty. We have been restored back to our place of power and dominion over all of creation. There should be no fear within us towards satan. The only limitation to us walking in that power is our lack of unity with the Holy Spirit. When we unite with the Holy Spirit we come into agreement with and experience the greatest power in the universe.

This is the type of power and dominion we are called to walk in. This is not some fantasy or false doctrine. This is the will of God concerning us. He's calling His people in this hour to rise up and walk in that which He's called us to in and through the Holy Spirit.

Bill Britton gives a powerful description of we, the people of God, walking in agreement with God-the Holy Spirit. And I say this prophetically, this is they type of man and woman of God that is about to manifest in the earth in the days to come:

> I want you to take a close look at this child of God... He walks continually under an anointing of the fulness of the Spirit. When he speaks, it is "thus saith the Lord," and settled in heaven. He has an unlimited vision into the unseen world, the thoughts of men's hearts are made manifest and nothing can be hidden from him. He does not preach for money, is not impressed by men of wealth, never pulls for an offering, yet has no lack and his efforts for the Kingdom are never slowed down for want of finances. He is not hindered by space or lack of transportation from one place to another, for he is caught away in the Spirit and transported to the place of need and ministry without time consuming and physically weary travel. He is never hindered from ministry by being laid up with sickness or physical ailments. At all times, yea twelve months out of the year, he bears an abundance of the Fruit of the Spirit. Joy flows from him like a river, Peace abides in his heart, and Love is as a great ocean.

The Power of Agreement

There is a continuous song of praise and victory on his lips, and never a complaint is heard. Nothing can cause him to become discouraged or lose heart. His faith never wavers. He has authority and dominion over everything made by the hand of God, and nothing can resist his word of power.

This person described is a person given over completely to the will and influence of the Holy Spirit. This is a person who walks in the fullness of God's character and nature, demonstrating the power and love of God in the earth and leading millions of souls to the Father because this person has realized that:

Can two walk together, except they be agreed?
Amos 3:3

God bless you.

www.ingramcontent.com/pod-product-compliance
Lightning Source LLC
LaVergne TN
LVHW091202080426
835509LV00006B/788